Opus 48

**Steidle + Partner
KPMG-Gebäude, München**

**Text
Wolfgang Bachmann**

**Photographien / Photographs
Reinhard Görner**

Edition Axel Menges

Herausgeber/Editor: Axel Menges

© 2003 Edition Axel Menges, Stuttgart/London
ISBN 3-930698-48-X

Alle Rechte vorbehalten, besonders die der Übersetzung in andere Sprachen.
All rights reserved, especially those of translation into other languages.

Reproduktionen: Reinhard Görner, Berlin
Druck/Printing: Druckhaus Münster GmbH, Kornwestheim
Bindearbeiten/Binding: Großbuchbinderei Fikentscher GmbH, Seeheim-Jugenheim

Design: Axel Menges
Übersetzung ins Englische/Translation into English: Michael Robinson

Inhalt

6   Wolfgang Bachmann: Das KPMG-Gebäude in München

20 Luftbild und Pläne
    Luftbild 20 – Lageplan 21 – Grundrisse 22 – Schnitte 26 – Fassadendetails 27

28 Bildteil
    Außenansichten 28 – Eingangsbereich 46 – Cafeteria 48 – Konferenzräume 50 – Haupttreppe 52 – Büros 58

60 Daten

Contents

7   Wolfgang Bachmann: The KPMG building in Munich

20 Aerial view and plans
    Aerial view 20 – Site plan 21 – Floor plans 22 – Sections 26 – Façade details 27

28 Pictorial section
    Exterior views 28 – Entrance area 46 – Cafeteria 48 – Conference rooms 50 – Main staircase 52 – Offices 58

60 Credits

Wolfgang Bachmann
Das KPMG-Gebäude in München

Den besten Blick hat man aus dem Café-Restaurant »Westend«, einem dieser Ecklokale mit großen Schaufenstern, wie sie vor allem in Berlin häufig anzutreffen sind: hohe Parketträume mit dunklem Gestühl und Wandspiegeln, die verläßlich die Mitte halten zwischen Biersalon und Kaffeehaus. Das entspricht auch dem zeitlosen Angebot der Speisekarte: Frühstück bis in die Puppen, gleichzeitig Pasta, Tex Mex und Braumeisterpfanne, Cocktails bis zum Abwinken. So stellt man sich auch hier in München die Großstadt vor. Das Haus mit der populären Kneipe ist ein grüngrauer Wohnblock, 1927/28 von den Architekten Eduard Herbert und Otho Orlando Kurz errichtet, eine solide Festung mit herrschaftlichen Eingängen aus Muschelkalk, martialischem Figurenschmuck und übereck reichenden Balkonbändern. Unter der Traufe schließt die Fassade mit einem Fries aus dreieckigen Fenstern, typisch für den Zeitgeschmack. Das Mietshaus daneben, ein wenig zurückhaltender inszeniert, wurde im gleichen Jahr von Theodor Fischer gebaut. Hans Kollhoff hätte seine Freude an diesen stattlichen Häusern, die an der Ganghoferstraße das neue Baugebiet auf der Theresienhöhe begrenzen.

Wenn man hier im Café »Westend« einen Fensterplatz ergattert hat, kann man beobachten, was auf der gegenüberliegenden Seite passiert. Noch ist die Straße von Baufahrzeugen beherrscht, zwischen den toten Trambahngleisen wuchern Huflattich, Rittersporn, Spitzwegerich und Sauerampfer. Die passable Breite von knapp 40 m verlangt nach einer urbanen Lösung: Genau in der Diagonale des Lokals steht ein aufsehenerregendes neues Bürogebäude, mit dessen blauer Leuchtschrift »KPMG« der Hausherr den Standort für sein Unternehmen reklamiert. Größer könnte der Gegensatz zu dem behäbigen Wohnungstrumm aus den späten zwanziger Jahren nicht sein. Während sich hier behaglich-monumental und erdverbunden eine deutsche Architektur artikuliert, bei der es ein Drinnen und Draußen gibt, eindeutige Ansichten (in vielerlei Hinsicht), ein Oben und Unten, gefügt in der Gewißheit auf den tradierten Verlauf der Geschichte, da antwortet gegenüber ein buntes, welsches Gerüst, das spielerisch eine Kubatur umschreibt, sich über der Traufe zurückfaltet, ohne aufzugeben, scheinbar allseitig wie eine Molekülstruktur weiter wachsen könnte, weil sein Bildungsgesetz so simpel erscheint, und nur, als sollte damit alle Hierarchie zum Narren gehalten werden, in seiner Mitte einen hochbeinigen, tempelartigen Eingang mit Ehrenhof anbietet. Die Fenster sind nur schmale Schlitze mit einer Mittelsprosse, alle zum Verwechseln gleich, wie von einer Maschine gestanzt; die Stützen und Deckenstürze, die endlos das Lochmuster im rechten Winkel zusammenhalten, sind in kräftige Farben getaucht, die wie geflochtene und gefaltete Papierbänder das tragende Skelett begleiten, als folgten sie einer geheimen Vereinbarung, als ließe sich damit eine Botschaft dechiffrieren, eine entartete Antwort auf die altdeutsche Idylle auf der anderen Straßenseite.

Daß diese Interpretation dem Architekten des Gebäudes gar nicht so fremd sein könnte, wird noch zu überprüfen sein. Hier innerhalb der sich vollendenden Neubebauung des ehemaligen Messegeländes geht es nicht in erster Linie um ein politisches Fanal, sondern um eine städtebauliche Ergänzung nach dem Wegzug der Messe, die ziemlich einmalig Wohnen, Arbeiten und Kultur miteinander verbindet. Sie ist das Ergebnis eines städtebaulichen Ideenwettbewerbs aus dem Jahr 1997, den Otto Steidle gewonnen hat. Einige Bauten, wie etwa das KPMG-Gebäude, konnte sein Büro selbst planen.

1. Bavariapark und Theresienwiese, München, 1920.
2. Steidle + Partner, Beitrag zum städtebaulichen Wettbewerb Theresienhöhe, 1997.

1. Bavariapark and Theresienwiese, Munich, 1920.
2. Steidle + Partner, entry to the Theresienhöhe town-planning competition, 1997.

Wolfgang Bachmann
The KPMG building in Munich

You get the best view from the »Westend« café-restaurant. It's one of those corner places with big windows, the sort you find in Berlin: high parquet rooms with dark-coloured seating and wall mirrors, a reliable halfway house between a beer hall and a coffee bar. The timeless menu fits in with this as well: breakfast till all hours, pasta, Tex Mex and fry-ups all at the same time, as many cocktails as you can drink. That's what Munich people think a big city should be like as well. The building containing this popular establishment is a grey-green residential block built in 1927/28 by the architects Eduard Herbert and Otho Orlando Kurz, a solid fortress with magnificent muschelkalk entrances, decorative martial figures and continuous balconies running round the corners. The façade concludes under the eaves with a frieze of triangular windows, typical of the taste of the period. The rather more reticent block of flats next door was built by Theodor Fischer in the same year. Hans Kollhoff would like these imposing buildings in Ganghoferstraße, marking the limits of the new building area on the Theresienhöhe.

Once you've managed to grab a window seat here in the »Westend« café you can watch what's going on at the other side of the road. The street is still dominated by contractors' vehicles, and coltsfoot, larkspur, ribwort and sorrel proliferate between the defunct tram tracks. The passable width of just under 40 m requires an urban solution. A striking new office building is going up exactly on the diagonal to the café, with its blue illuminated »KPMG« sign advertising the site for its company. There could hardly be a greater contrast with the large, solid, late 20s residential monsters. These are comfortably monumental and earth-bound, a clear statement by a kind of German architecture that has an inside and an outside, unambiguous aspects (in many ways), a top and a bottom, put together in the certainty that history will run its traditional course. The response from opposite is a brightly coloured alien framework, playfully defining a cubic volume that folds back over the eaves without giving in, seeming as though it could grow on all sides like a molecular structure because it is built to such simple rules. But then, as though to ridicule any sense of hierarchy, in the middle is a long-legged, temple-like entrance with a court of honour. The windows are just narrow slits with a central bar, all completely alike, as if stamped out by a machine; the supports and ceiling lintels, endlessly keeping up the perforated pattern at right angles, are painted in strong colours and accompany the load-bearing skeleton like woven and folded strips of paper, as though keeping to some secret agreement, as though they are a way of deciphering a message, a degenerate response to the old German idyll opposite.

We shall see later whether the architect of the building might find this interpretation not particularly strange. Here, inside the new development of the former exhibition site, which is now drawing to a close, the main aim is not to produce a political beacon, but to complete a piece of urban development after the departure of the exhibition centre, combining housing, work and culture in a pretty unique way. It is the result of an urban development competition dating from 1997, and won by Otto Steidle. His own office was allowed to plan some buildings, like the KPMG building, for example.

Time to get up

When the warehouse worker August Kühn was looking for somewhere to live here on the Schwanthaler Höhe after the Franco-Prussian War, a lot of the street names

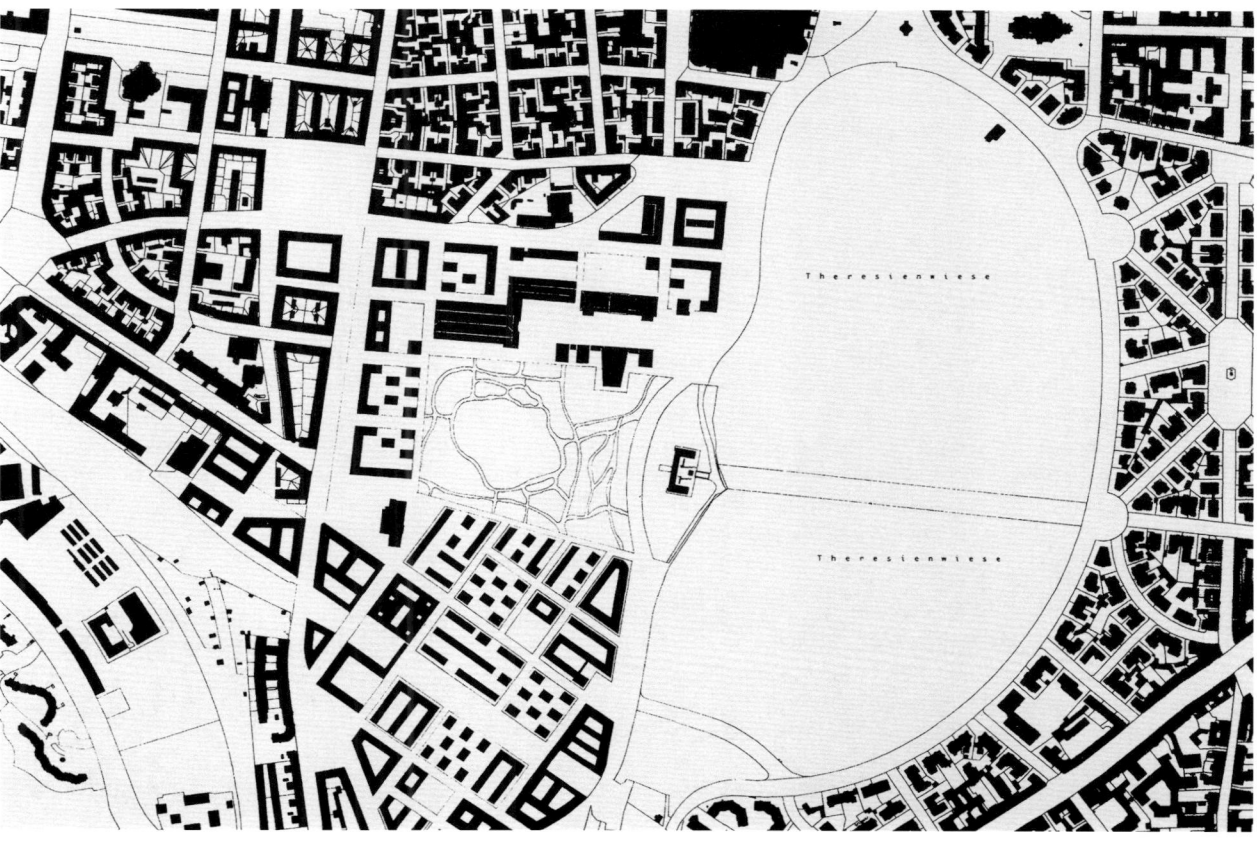

Zeit zum Aufstehn

Als der Güterhallenarbeiter August Kühn nach dem Deutsch-Französichen Krieg hier auf der Schwanthaler Höhe eine Bleibe suchte, gab es schon viele der noch heute gültigen Straßennamen, benannt nach »Kazmair, Ridler, Ligsalz und Tulbeck ..., im Mittelalter die Großen, die Familien, die ... für den Herzog Geldgeber für Sonderprivilegien geworden waren, mit denen sie die unteren Stände und Zünfte vom Mitreden im Rat ausschlossen« – politisch richtungsweisender Auftakt des Arbeiterromans *Zeit zum Aufstehn*, in dem Helmuth-Hans Münch unter dem Pseudonym seines Helden Ort und Milieu der »roten« Schwanthaler Höhe bis in die siebziger Jahre des 20. Jahrhunderts nachzeichnet.

Armselig waren Verhältnisse und Wohnbedingungen, aber es gab schon die von Leo von Klenze errichtete Ruhmeshalle mit dem begehbaren Riesenstandbild der Bavaria, ein vaterländisches Monument, im Gegensatz zur nationalen Walhalla bei Regensburg »zum Ruhme der verdienten und besonders ausgezeichneten Bayern« von Ludwig I. erdacht. Den idyllischen Park mit seinen Steinplastiken, der heute den Maklern als überzeugendes, unbezahlbares Argument für die Wohnungen und Büroflächen dient, gab es damals noch nicht. Die Schlafstellenvermieterin von August Kühn sammelte hier »Klaubholz, oft auf dem Rücken einer Kuh, aus dem Auwald hinter der Bavaria«.

Erst um 1907/08 entstand unter der Federführung von Wilhelm Bertsch, dem Leiter des Stadtbauamts, der »Münchner Ausstellungspark«, bei dessen Planung bekannte einheimische Architekten wie die Brüder von Seidl mitwirkten. 1934 als Vergnügungspark geschlossen, wurde die Grünanlage mehr und mehr für den Ausbau der Messe in Anspruch genommen. Nach dem Krieg, mit der Gründung der Münchner Messe- und Ausstellungsgesellschaft, gelang der eigentliche Durchbruch zu einem internationalen Messeplatz, der neben den noch vom Jugendstil geprägten, heute unter Denkmalschutz stehenden Hallen ein Sammelsurium weiterer Großbauten im Zeitgeschmack ihres Baujahrs entstehen ließ. 1972 kam mit der vorübergehend als Ringerhalle für die Olympischen Spiele genutzten Arena eine weitere Doppelhalle dazu. Im Jahr 1983 war mit der Überbauung der Bahnanlagen schließlich die maximale Kapazität des Geländes erreicht.

Dieser Park, in dessen Nähe einige historische Villen standen, bildet die eigentliche Theresienhöhe oberhalb der »Wiesn«, dem Austragungsort des weltbekannten Oktoberfests. Ende des 19. Jahrhunderts galt die Gegend als eines der vornehmsten Wohnquartiere Münchens. Das Haupthaus der Villa von Georg Joseph von Hauberrisser, unter anderem Architekt des Neuen Rathauses, steht heute städtebaulich isoliert im Norden der Festwiese. Die Stein gewordene Geschichte demonstriert, wie vielfältig und uneinheitlich sich das attraktive Baugebiet nächst Bahnhof und Zentrum entwickelt hat.

Ein ganz besonderer Wettbewerb

Diese soziale Melange verlangte bei dem städtebaulichen Wettbewerb eine angemessene Antwort. Dazu formierten sich umgehend Bürgerinitiativen, die eine fremde Bebauung mit Luxuswohnungen und smarten Büros befürchteten. Der zunächst diskutierte »Kulturschwerpunkt« mit naturkundlichem Bildungszentrum, Haus der Musik, Kunsthalle, Musicaltheater und dergleichen war »aus finanziellen Gründen« bereits weitgehend aufgegeben. Hatte die Stadtbaurätin Christiane Thalgott 1995 noch die Meßlatte hoch gelegt (»Das muß etwas ganz Besonderes werden und darf nicht für den Alltag verbraucht werden«), zeigt heute die Mischung von Wohnen und Gewerbe genau das Alltägliche – das man allerdings in der sich andeutenden Qualität gern erwartet. Im nachhinein amüsiert es sogar, an welchen hochfliegenden Plänen sich die Politik erwärmt, wenn sich dazu Gelegenheit bietet. Schließlich gilt speziell für München, daß die Stadt, die auf der Beliebtheitsskala ganz oben steht, nichts mehr als attraktives Bauland benötigt. Das hat sich in den letzten Jahren allerdings planmäßig vermehrt, nachdem Industrie und Gewerbe an die Peripherie abgewandert sind, Kasernen geschlossen, Güterbahnhof und Flughafen verlegt wurden und die Messe auf das frei gewordene Gelände in Riem gezogen ist. Damit wurde auch die Theresienhöhe zur städtebaulichen Entwicklungsfläche.

Nach kontroverser Diskussion in einem vom städtischen Planungsreferat mit großer Bürgerbeteiligung veranstalteten Workshop erwartete man von den Wettbewerbsteilnehmern – zehn Büros aus einer Vorauswahl von 138 Interessenten – »ein in sich geschlossenes Quartier ..., das die Strukturen der alten gewachsenen Stadtteile drumherum aufgreift, aber dem Ganzen einen modernen Ausdruck gibt«, so Camilla Will, die Projektleiterin der Stadt. Das Verfahren war kein anonymer Ideenwettbewerb, sondern eine offene Kooperation mit vier gemeinsamen Arbeitssitzungen. Am Ergebnis fiel auf, daß zwei nachhaltig mit München vertraute Büros – Steidle + Partner und Hilmer & Sattler – den ersten bzw. zweiten Platz erreichten – und zwar mit völlig gegensätzlichen Vorschlägen. Der dritte Preis ging an Ortner & Ortner, Berlin.

Konkurrierende Stadtbilder

Das Büro Hilmer & Sattler wurde für einen erstaunlichen städtebaulichen Vorschlag ausgezeichnet, der sich eher an der historischen Bebauung an der Ganghoferstraße orientiert. Es befestigte die etwa 8 m über der Theresienwiese liegende Hangkante auf beiden Seiten des Bavariaparks mit einer dem Straßenverlauf folgenden, sehr langen Wohnwand, die an großstädtische Formen der zwanziger Jahre erinnerte, in München an dieser Stelle aber ein Fremdkörper gewesen wäre. Noch kurioser nahmen sich die C- und U-förmigen Blöcke aus, die sich krampfartig zusammenzogen und mit Eckbastionen gesichert waren, als hätten die Bewohner etwas zu verteidigen – eine leichtfertige Anspielung, wenn man sich an die von August Kühn literarisch überlieferten Arbeiterkämpfe in diesem Viertel erinnert. Zwar ist ein Ideenwettbewerb kein realistischer Bebauungsplan, aber es verwundert, wenn ein prämierter Vorschlag so weit entfernt von einem wünschenswerten Stadtquartier ansetzt. Vom »Arbeitskreis Theresienhöhe«, einem monatlich tagenden offenen Diskussionsforum aus Mitgliedern der Bezirksausschüsse und verschiedener Bürgerinitiativen, wurde der Beitrag als der am wenigsten geeignete aller zehn Entwürfe eingestuft, nachdem das Planungsreferat ihn für kurze Zeit in die Überlegungen für den Bebauungsplan einbezogen hatte. Schließlich überzeugte der Entwurf des ersten Preisträgers Steid-

3, 4. Steidle + Partner, Internationales Begegnungszentrum, Berlin, 1979–83. (Photos: Verena von Gagern.)

that are still in use today were already in place. They were named after »Kazmaier, Ridler, Ligsalz and Tulbeck …, the great medieval families, who … had provided money for the Duke in exchange for special privileges, which they used to exclude the lower classes and the guilds from having their say in the council« – this is the politically significant start to the workers' novel *Zeit zum Aufstehn* (Time to get up), in which Helmut Hans Münch, writing under the pseudonym of his hero, followed the fortunes of the »red« Schwanthaler Höhe as a location and milieu until the 1970s.

The circumstances and living conditions were impoverished, but Leo von Klenze's Hall of Fame with its gigantic accessible statue of Bavaria was already in place, a monument to the fatherland, unlike the national Valhalla near Regensburg, erected by Ludwig I »to the glory of outstanding and especially distinguished Bavarians«. The idyllic park with its stone statues, which estate agents use today as a convincing and attractive argument for the flats and office spaces, did not exist at that time. Here August Kühn's landlady who let sleeping space used to collect »firewood, often on the back of a cow, from the riverside woodland behind the Bavaria«.

It was not until 1907/08, under Wilhelm Bertsch, the director of the municipal building office, that the »Munich Exhibition Park« came into being; well-known local architects like the von Seidl brothers were involved in the planning process. The green area was closed as a pleasure park in 1934, and then used more and more to develop the exhibition centre. After the war, when the Munich Trade Fair and Exhibition Company was founded, movement towards an international exhibition centre really got under way. This led to the emergence of a motley collection of other large buildings following contemporary taste alongside the older halls, now listed, which were still very much in the spirit of Jugendstil. Another double hall, the arena used temporarily as a wrestling hall for the Olympic games, was added in 1972. The site reached its maximum capacity in 1983, when the railway lines were built over.

This park, which had some historic villas nearby, forms the actual Theresienhöhe above the »Wiesn« (meadows) where the world-famous Oktoberfest is held. In the late 19th century the area was seen as one of Munich's most desirable residential areas. The main section of Georg Joseph von Hauberrisser's villa – he was the architect of the Neues Rathaus, among other things – now stand to the north of the Oktoberfest site, isolated in urban terms. History has turned to stone, demonstrating how diversely and with what lack of unity this attractive building land next to the station and the centre has developed.

A very special competition

This social mixture required an appropriate response from the urban development competition. Citizens' initiatives sprang up immediately, fearing an alien development with luxury housing and smart offices. The »cultural focal point«, with a nature education centre, concert hall, art gallery, musical theatre and things of the like had already been largely abandoned »for financial reasons«. Although building councillor Christiane Thalgott may still have been speaking out for high architectural standards in 1995 (»That must come out as some-

thing very special and must not be used up for ordinary purposes«), the present mixture of housing and commerce shows precisely that ordinariness – though it can be eagerly anticipated, given the quality that seems to be emerging. In retrospect it is even quite amusing to see how enthusiastic politicians can get about high-flying plans if the opportunity presents itself. And ultimately it is absolutely true of Munich, which is very high up on the popularity scale as a city, that it needs nothing more than attractive building land. Though of course there has been more of it about in recent years, now that industry and commerce have moved to the periphery, barracks have been closed down, the freight station and the airport moved and the exhibition centre has moved out to the site that was freed up in Riem. This also made the Theresienhöhe into an urban-development area.

After heated discussions at a workshop arranged by the municipal planning department, in which a large number of the public took part, what was expected from the competition entrants – ten offices from a long list of 138 interested parties – was »a quarter that is complete in itself …, that takes up the structures of the old, mature districts around it, but gives the whole project a sense of modernity«, in the words of Camilla Will, the project director for the city. The procedure was not an anonymous ideas competition, but an open co-operation, with four joint working sessions. An interesting feature of the result was that two practices with a great deal of experience of Munich – Steidle + Partner and Hilmer & Sattler – won the first and second prizes respectively – and with suggestions that were complete opposites. The third prize went to Ortner & Ortner, Berlin.

Competing cityscapes

Hilmer & Sattler were commended for an astonishing urban proposal that draws more from the historical development in Ganghoferstraße. It fixed the sloping periphery on both sides of the Bavariapark about 8 m above the Theresienwiese with a very long residential wall following the line of the streets. This is reminiscent of the city forms prevalent in the twenties, but it would have been a foreign body on this site in Munich. The C- and U-shaped blocks seemed even more curious: these drew themselves together convulsively and were secured with corner bastions, as though the residents had something to defend – an ill-considered allusion if we remember the workers' fights in this quarter that have come down to us in August Kühn's writings. Of course an ideas competition of this nature is not intended to be a realistic development plan, but it is surprising when a winning proposal starts off at such a distance from a desirable urban quarter. The »Theresienhöhe working group«, an open discussion forum made up of members of the district committees and various citizens' initiatives, ranked this entry as the least suitable of all then ten submitted after the planning department had included it in the considerations for the development plan for a short time. Ultimately everyone was persuaded by the design by the first prizewinners, Steidle + Partner, from which the matrix that is being followed by today's construction unmistakably developed.

This development proposal, which used the façade colours of the later KPMG building even in the urban development submission, in favourable anticipation,

le + Partner, aus dem sich unverkennbar die Matrix entwickelte, nach der heute gebaut wird.

Dieser Bebauungvorschlag, der bereits in der städtebaulichen Darstellung sympathisch vorauseilend die Fassadenfarben des späteren KPMG-Gebäudes benutzte, zeigt ein charmantes Nebeneinander von Ordnung und Freiheit, von Baublöcken und Punkthäusern. Manfred Sack nannte ihn in der Wochenzeitung *Die Zeit* »einen festen, räumlich intelligenten, mannigfaltigen, sehr städtischen Entwurf«.

Zwei Raster, zwei Fluchten

Für Steidle bedeutet Städtebau keine neue, andere Disziplin, sondern wie Architektur ein konkretes Konstrukt zwischen Bauen und Leben. In einem Interview führte er einmal aus: »Ich möchte eine Architektur machen, die städtisch ist. Nicht nur etwa im typologischen Sinne, sondern städtisch in sich selbst, städtisch im Sinne der Nutzung, der Aneignung. Ich meine eine Architektur, die unterschiedliche Räume ausbildet – Gassen, Höfe, Straßen – und gleichzeitig Zwischenzonen, die gar nicht so genau definiert sind.«

Seine Überzeugung, daß zuerst das Ganze stimmen muß, bevor man sich den Details widmet – die vielleicht gar nicht so wichtig sind, auf jeden Fall sich nicht verselbständigen dürfen, nur weil es das Leistungsbild des Architekten so vorsieht –, ist an diesem Plan beispielhaft ablesbar. Steidle hat sich mit keiner wissenschaftlichen Grundsatzarbeit gequält, sondern bis in die Darstellung der Idee mit dem Naheliegenden, dem Sichtbaren gearbeitet. »Otto Steidle ist ein bebilderter Mensch. Er nimmt Bilder in sich auf, eigene wie fremde, sucht und findet Bilder, die die eigenen Vorstellungen verdeutlichen und belegen«, schrieb Florian Kossak in einer 1994 erschienenen Monographie über den Architekten. Und es ließ sich regelmäßig bei wesentlich kleineren Arbeiten feststellen, daß das Büro die Gabe besitzt, eine erfaßte Situation stimmig weiter zu interpretieren. Dazu zählen die kleine Bebauung am Wittelsbacher Rondell in München (1980/81), die sich charmant in eine großbürgerliche Villenumgebung fügt, und die vielgerühmte Architektur des Internationalen Begegnungszentrums in Berlin-Wilmersdorf (1979–83), die ebenfalls im Charakter des Quartiers weiter wächst.

So läßt auch Steidles Vorschlag für die Theresienhöhe erkennen, daß jemand nicht bloß eine Ausschreibung gelesen hat, um danach eigenwillig die geforderten Baumassen zu verteilen, sondern daß er den unbeschreibbaren Ton eines Ortes begriffen hat. Vielleicht ein Vorteil, der sich aus der lebensnahen, immer wieder mit dem Pragmatischen konfrontierten Vita des Bauernbubs aus Milbertshofen herleiten läßt? Doch sollte man sich nicht als Hobbypsychologe versuchen, um zu erklären, warum manche Architekten für bestimmte Aufgaben ein besonderes Talent entwickeln. Auch ohne Spekulation kann man an Steidles Zeichnung ablesen, wie sich aus den beiden Hauptfluchten des Planungsgebiets, zuerst der nördlichen Kante des Bavariaparks, dann der diagonal einschneidenden Flucht der Bahnlinie, eine spannende Ordnung ergibt. Die beiden Koordinaten-Richtungen treffen sich am Standort der alten Feuerwache, die zu einem Jugendzentrum umgebaut werden wird. Selten hat man einen Plan gesehen, der sich so wenig auf romantische Tümelei einläßt, aber gleichzeitig keine strenge Räson, kein gnadenloses Raster vorzeichnet, nach dem die künftige Bebauung einschraffiert werden soll. Sie wird vielmehr mit den größeren Gebäuden an den Kanten und den kleineren im Zentrum der einzelnen Blöcke eine Ahnung der nächsten Umgebung weitergeben. Das versetzte Feld für die Punkthäuser könnte als ein auf den Baugrund projizierter Fassadenplan aus dem aktuellen Architekturrepertoire gelesen werden. Die Jury nannte es einen »gelungenen Versuch, eine neue stadträumliche Struktur für das ehemalige Messegelände aus dem Modul der umliegenden Quartiere zu formulieren, ohne diese jedoch zu kopieren«. Sie lobte die Möglichkeit, sukzessive die Architektur unterschiedlicher Handschriften zu erlauben, ohne den Maßstab und die Identität des neuen Stadtteils zu gefährden. Die Neutralität der Grundstruktur lasse ohne Schwierigkeiten den Wechsel von Nutzungsbeziehungen im Laufe der Realisierung zu – was ja bereits passiert.

Die Schönheit der Stadt

Der Standort für das spätere KPMG-Gebäude und das dahinter liegende Wohnhochhaus war bereits umschrieben, allerdings sollte sich der Entwurf noch einige Male ändern, bevor das heutige Ensemble sichtbar wurde. Zunächst erhielten Steidle + Partner einen Beratervertrag, mit dem sie die Stadt während der Aufstellung des Bebauungsplans begleiteten. Auf dieser Grundlage wurden für die Schule und ein weiteres Baufeld mit drei Wohnhäusern an der Heimeranstraße offene Wettbewerbe ausgelobt; bei den übrigen Baufeldern galt für die Grundstückskäufer die Bedingung, entweder die drei ausgezeichneten Architekturbüros des städtebaulichen Wettbewerbs gemeinsam zu berücksichtigen oder in einem neuen offenen Workshop einen Bebauungsvorschlag eines anderen Architekten kennenzulernen und weiterzuverfolgen. KPMG, ein international tätiges Wirtschaftsprüfungs- und Beratungsunternehmen, das hier auf der Theresienhöhe der einzige Eigennutzer unter den Bauherren ist, entschied sich für die zweite Möglichkeit. Eingeladen zu dem Workshop wurden außer Steidle + Partner die Büros Herman Hertzberger aus Amsterdam, Adolf Krischanitz aus Wien, Schneider + Schumacher aus Frankfurt, Degle Gesellschaft von Architekten aus Königsbrunn sowie die Arbeitsgemeinschaft Rudolf Hierl und Amann & Gittel Architekten aus München. Entwerfen unter Hochdruck – das KPMG-Projekt wurde an einem konzentrierten, schlaflosen Wochenende von den konkurrierenden Kollegen entwickelt – scheint eine besondere Leistungsklasse des Büros Steidle + Partner zu sein.

Erstaunlich liest sich in der Dokumentation des Verfahrens, wie weit sich der Bauherr auf die städtebauliche Situation eingelassen hat, auf den Erhalt der gewachsenen Stadtstrukturen und die Kontinuität der vorhandenen Grünflächen. Die Stadt München, repräsentiert durch ihre Stadtbaurätin Christiane Thalgott, operierte vor allem mit dem Begriff »hochwertig«. Damit ist nicht gemeint, daß auf der Theresienhöhe besonders teure, exklusive Architektur, sondern nach dem Wegzug der Messe ein sehr attraktives, zentrumsnahes Quartier entstehen soll, das man nicht einem Grundstückverwertungsunternehmen überlassen will. Dazu muß man die widersprüchlichen Interessen so lenken, daß das Kapital investiert und der kleine Bürger sich nicht betrogen vorkommt. Also eine Standard-Aufga-

5. Steidle + Partner, KPMG-Gebäude. München. Modell.
6. Adolf Krischanitz, KPMG-Gebäude, München. Modell.
7. Herman Hertzberger, KPMG-Gebäude, München. Modell.

5. Steidle + Partner, KPMG building. Munich. Model.
6. Adolf Krischanitz, KPMG building. Munich. Model.
7. Herman Hertzberger, KPMG building. Munich. Model.

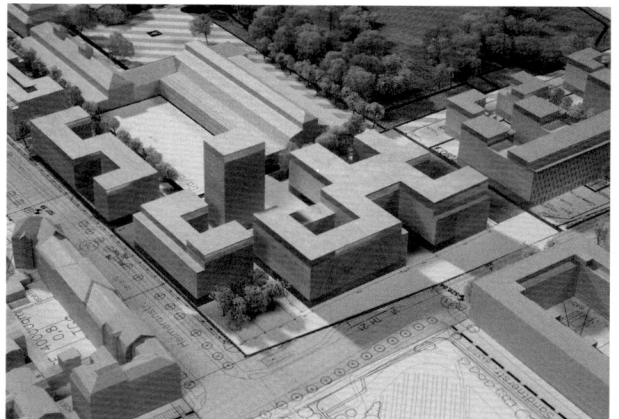

shows a charming juxtaposition of order and freedom, of blocks and point buildings. Writing in the weekly newspaper *Die Zeit*, Manfred Sack called it »a solid, spatially intelligent, diverse, very urban design«.

Two grids, two building lines

For Steidle, urban development is not a new, different discipline, but like architecture a concrete construct placed somewhere between building and life. He once stated in an interview: »I should like to make a kind of urban architecture. Not just typologically, but urban in itself, urban in the sense of use, of appropriation. I mean a kind of architecture that creates a variety of spaces – alleyways, courtyards, streets – and at the same time intermediate zones that are not so precisely defined.«

His conviction that the plan as a whole has to be right before turning to the details – which are perhaps not so important, in any case they shouldn't make themselves independent simply because the architect's targets see it like that – can be seen in an exemplary way in this plan. Steidle did not torment himself with academic groundwork, but worked with what was obvious and visible, right down to representing the idea itself. »Otto Steidle is an illustrated man. He absorbs images, his own and others, looks for and finds images that clarify and support his own ideas«, wrote Florian Kossak in a monograph about the architect published in 1994. And crucial small works regularly showed that his practice has the gift of continuing to interpret a situation consistently once they have grasped it. Examples include the small development at the Wittelsbacher Rondell in Munich (1980/81), which fits in charmingly in an upper middle-class villa district, and the much praised architecture of the Internationales Begegnungszentrum in Wilmersdorf, Berlin (1979–83), which also keeps on growing into the character of the quarter.

So Steidle's proposal for the Theresienhöhe shows that this was not just a case of someone reading a competition brief and then disposing the required building masses just as he feels like it, but that he has grasped the indescribable tone of a place. Is this perhaps an advantage derived from the closeness to life of this farm lad from Milbertshofen, who has always been confronted with the pragmatic? But it shouldn't be necessary to try one's skill as an amateur psychologist to explain why certain architects develop a particular talent for certain jobs. But without any sort of speculation it is possible to discern from Steidle's drawing how he has taken the two main building lines of the planning area, first the northern periphery of the Bavariapark and then the diagonal incision made by the railway line to produce an exciting sense of order. The two co-ordinates meet at the site of the old fire station, which is to be rebuilt as a youth centre. It is rare to see a plan that is so little tempted to romantic flights but at the same time does not insist on rigid rationality or a pitiless grid onto which all the rest of the future development has to be hatched. In fact the development will be much more likely to pass on an idea of the immediate vicinity, with the larger buildings on the periphery and the larger ones in the centre of the individual blocks. The staggered field for the point buildings could be read as a façade plan from the current architectural repertoire, projected onto the plot. The jury called it a »successful attempt to formulate a new urban structure for the exhibition ground from the module of the surrounding quarters, but without copying them«. It praised the possibility of successively permitting the architecture to have different handwriting, without endangering the scale and the identity of the new urban district. They went on to say that the neutral quality of the basic structure meant that it was not difficult to change the way uses relate to each other in the course of realization – which indeed is already happening.

The beauty of the city

The site for the what was to become the KPMG building and the high-rise block of flats behind it had already been fixed, though the design was to change a few more times before the present ensemble became visible. At first Steidle + Partner were commissioned to act as consultants to the city while the development plan was being put in place. Open competitions were announced on this basis for the school and another building plot with three housing blocks in Heimeranstraße; for the other plots, buyers were required either to consider the three prizewinning architectural practices from the urban development competition, or to familiarize themselves with a development proposal by another architect in a new open workshop, and then to pursue it further. KPMG, the international accountants and consultants, the only owner-user among the firms building on the Theresienhöhe, decided on the second alternative. As well as Steidle + Partner, they invited Herman Hertzberger from Amsterdam, Adolf Krischanitz from Vienna, Schneider + Schumacher from Frankfurt, Degle Gesellschaft von Architekten from Königsbrunn and the Rudolf Hierl und Amann & Gittel Architekten co-operative from Munich to the workshop. Design under pressure – the KPMG project was developed in one concentrated, sleepless weekend by the competing colleagues – this seems to be something of a Steidle + Partner speciality.

It is astonishing to read in the records of the proceedings how much KPMG accepted the urban situation and the fact that they had to preserve naturally matured urban structures and the continuity of the existing green spaces. The city of Munich, represented by its building councillor Christiane Thalgott, used the word »high calibre« a great deal. This did not mean that she wanted to see especially expensive, exclusive architecture on the Theresienhöhe, but that the intention was to build a very attractive quarter near the centre after the exhibition centre moved out, and they did not want to lose it to an ordinary property-development company. In order to do this, the conflicting interests have to be guided so that capital is invested and the man in the street does not feel let down. In other words a standard brief from a successful red-green city government using key words like »compact – urban – green«. An additional factor in this case is that unlike other current urban projects there is a challenge from what could be called the special Munich situation. At last it is possible to build up the beauty of the city again, not just mass housing construction on faceless peripheral industrial sites, no closing up gaps between backyard buildings. There is a suggestion that the broad Ganghoferstraße could be enhanced as an »esplanade«, a favourite Postmodern term originally picked up from fortress ar-

benstellung für eine erfolgreiche rot-grüne Stadtregierung, die mit den Leitvokabeln »kompakt – urban – grün« angetreten ist. In diesem Fall kommt noch hinzu, daß im Gegensatz zu anderen aktuellen städtischen Projekten die besondere, münchnerisch zu nennende Situation herausfordert. Endlich läßt sich einmal an der Schönheit der Stadt weiterbauen, kein Massenwohnungsbau auf gesichtslosen Industriearealen an der Peripherie, keine Lückenschließung zwischen Hinterhäusern. Für die breite Ganghoferstraße bietet sich die Aufwertung zu einer »Esplanade« an, ein postmodern gepflegter Begriff aus dem Festungsbau, den man von Steidles südlich an das KPMG-Gebäude anschließenden Bürobauten übernommen hat. Der Boulevard ruft. Mit den braven Wohnhäusern des Arbeiterviertels Westend hat das dann nichts mehr zu tun. Man darf gespannt sein, wie die Blockrandbebauung der zwanziger Jahre, die heute von vielen Architekten wieder geschätzt wird, und die neuen Bürowelten zusammenwachsen werden.

Adolf Krischanitz betonte in seinem Beitrag zumindest verbal die Brüche solcher Nicht-Orte, Herausforderungen, für die es wichtig ist, »daß man sie urban formuliert«. Herman Hertzberger schlug – nicht unerwartet – relativ kleine Baukörper vor, die sich zu größeren Gebäuden zusammenfassen lassen, aber auch selbständig genutzt werden können. Wichtig sind die sich ergebenden Zwischenzonen: »Die Trennräume bestehen aus öffentlichen und semiöffentlichen Freiflächen und deformieren gewissermaßen die regelmäßige Bebauungsstruktur.« Otto Steidle dagegen setzte auf die Harmonie; nach seiner Meinung »soll die ganze Theresienhöhe grundsätzlich ein homogenes Stadtquartier werden, bei dem sich Wohn- und Bürohäuser per se nicht unterscheiden, das heißt nicht zwingend vom Maßstab und Ausdruck her auf Gegensatz arbeiten, sondern tendenziell auf Vereinheitlichung«. Es ist die Idee, die ihn schon bei seinem letzten großen Münchner Projekt, dem Wacker-Haus an der Prinzregentenstraße (1992 bis 1997) interessiert hat. Teure Büroflächen in Wohnungen umzuwidmen, läßt sich zwar mit der Architektur lösen. Ob sich, wenn die Arbeit ausgeht, für teure Wohnflächen überhaupt noch Mieter finden lassen, ist eine andere Frage. Hier geht es aber zunächst einmal um ein urbanes Nebeneinander und keine Rückbaupläne für Krisenzeiten. Vor allem ein Wohnturm, Reminiszenz an den 1970 abgebrochenen Messeturm und deshalb von der Stadt als Beitrag zu den baugeschichtlichen Memorabilien begrüßt, wird über den Büros für die vitale Anwesenheit von Menschen sorgen. Zum eigentlichen KPMG-Gebäude, einem großen, im Grundriß mäandrierenden Bauwerk, das fast bis zur Heimeranstraße reicht und den Wohnturm umklammert, führt Steidle aus: »Ein keramikverkleidetes Skelett, welches sich als Gefüge in der Perspektive schließt. Durch etwa Dreiviertel Glasanteil ist orthogonal gesehen die Transparenz vorherrschend. Die Fensterlaibungen sind farbig gestaltet und zeigen in den einzelnen Bereichen unterschiedliche Farben. So wird über den Körper mit seinen differenzierten Höfen eine sowohl transparente als auch stabile – und farbige Akzentuierung erreicht. Diese Stelle am Eingang zum Westend und am alten Messeviertel wird so im Sinne des beabsichtigten Gesamtquartiers definiert.« Bis auf die Front an der Ganghoferstraße entsprach dieser Entwurf den Vorstellungen der Jury. Teile der Bearbeitung sollten den Verfas-

8. Steidle+Partner, Michaelis-Quartier, Hamburg, 1994 bis 2001. (Photo: Petra Steiner.)
9. Steidle+Partner, KPMG-Gebäude München, 1995 bis 2002. (Photo: Reinhard Görner.)

8. Steidle+Partner, Michaelis-Quartier, Hamburg, 1994 to 2001. (Photo: Pertra Steiner.)
9. Steidle+Partner, KPMG building, Munich, 1995 to 2002. (Photo: Reinhard Görner.)

chitecture and taken over from Steidle's office buildings adjacent to the KPMG building to the south. The call of the boulevard. This will then have nothing in common with the worthy housing in the working-class Westend district. It will be very interesting to see how the twenties block periphery developments, which a lot of architects value highly again today, and the new office worlds will mature and blend together.

In his contribution, Adolf Krischanitz emphasized, at least verbally, the fractures that are to be found in these non-places, challenges that it is important »to formulate them in an urban way«. Herman Hertzberger suggested – not unexpectedly – relatively small building sections that could come together to form larger structures, but could also be used independently. The intermediate zones that emerge are important here: »The dividing spaces consist of public and semi-public open areas that distort the regular development structure to a certain extent. But Otto Steidle was determined to go for harmony; he felt that »the whole of the Theresienhöhe should fundamentally become a homogeneous urban quarter in which there is no distinction as such between housing and offices, in other words there was no compulsion to work on contrasts derived from scale and expression, but to look for unity quite deliberately«. This was the idea that interested him particularly in his last major project in Munich, the Wacker-Haus in Prinzregentenstraße (1992–97). Converting expensive office space into dwellings is a problem that can be solved by architecture. But the question is: if work is running short, will it be possible to find tenants for expensive housing? This is all about urban juxtaposition in the first place, and not a secure means of retreat at times of crisis. A residential tower block in particular will be reminiscent of the exhibition centre tower that was pulled down in 1970, and will therefore be welcomed by the city as a contribution to the memorabilia of building history; it will also deal with the vital presence of people above the offices. On the subject of the actual KPMG building, a large structure with a meandering ground plan extending almost as far as Heimeranstraße and clasping the high-rise block, Steidle stated: »A ceramic-clad skeleton, fitting in with the perspective as a structure. Given the proportions of three-quarters glass, transparency is the dominant factor orthogonally. The window reveals are coloured differently in the various sectors. Thus a sense of transparent, stable – and indeed coloured accentuation is achieved via the body of the building with its differentiated courtyards. Thus this point at the entrance to the suburb of Westend by the old exhibition ground is defined in the spirit of the quarter as a whole.« This design met the jury's requirements, with the exception of the façade in Ganghoferstraße. Some of the work was to be transferred to the authors of the works in second place – the Hertzberger and Krischanitz practices.

But other reasons tipped the balance here as well. As KPMG did not want to play the client role themselves and were also interested in the amount of office space they needed for their own use, the firm commissioned Investa to develop the project along with the housing required by the city. This resulted in another change to the development proposal that had been devised; the tower block was detached from the cubature of the building and the housing and office development extending to the corner of the block, which Adolf Krischanitz was working on further, was defined as a building in its own right. It has to be admitted that this continuation, triggered by pragmatic conditions, gave the project a clearer outline.

A sense of community, a sense of self and urban space

In his new book *Verhaltene Geschwindigkeit*, Vittorio Magnago Lampugnani writes: »The architectural structures of the city can … no longer keep pace with those of the new organization of work; consequently they have to become so neutral that they can accommodate the changes that are to be anticipated but not predicted precisely without having to suffer expensive structural

sern der zweitrangigen Arbeiten – dem Büro Hertzberger bzw. dem Büro Krischanitz – übertragen werden.

Dafür waren noch andere Gründe ausschlaggebend. Da KPMG nicht selbst Bauherr spielen wollte und sich auch nur für den Eigenbedarf an Büroflächen (28 000 m²) interessierte, beauftragte sie die Firma Investa, das Projekt samt dem von der Stadt geforderten Wohnungsbau (12 000 m²) abzuwickeln. Das führte dazu, daß sich der erarbeitete Bebauungsvorschlag noch einmal wandelte: Der Wohnturm wurde von der Gebäudekubatur abgelöst, die Wohn- und Bürobebauung bis zur Blockecke, die Adolf Krischanitz weiterbearbeitete, wurde als eigenständiges Haus definiert. Man muß zugeben, daß diese von pragmatischen Bedingungen ausgelöste Fortschreibung dem Projekt eine deutlichere Kontur gegeben hat.

Gemeinsinn, Eigensinn und urbaner Raum

In seinem jüngst erschienen Buch *Verhaltene Geschwindigkeit* schreibt Vittorio Magnago Lampugnani: »Die baulichen Strukturen der Stadt können ... nicht mehr mit jenen der neuen Arbeitsorganisation Schritt halten; folglich müssen sie so neutral werden, daß sie den zu erwartenden, aber nicht genau voraussehbaren Wandel aufnehmen können, ohne aufwendige bauliche Eingriffe zu erleiden. Das bedeutet nichts anderes, als daß die Bürohäuser in der Stadt dauerhafter geplant und gebaut werden müssen als bisher. Und daß sie sich weniger nach den Nutzungen richten müssen und können, die sie aufzunehmen haben, als nach ihrer Situierung im urbanen Raum.« Es könnte ein Merksatz für das KPMG-Gebäude sein, obwohl das Dauerhafte, Repräsentative, Unveränderliche nicht zu den Leitvokabeln in Steidles Architektur-Merkbuch gehören.

Am Anfang von Steidles Praxis standen der Wohnungsbau und die Suche nach dem, was den Menschen fördernd umgeben könnte. Es war ihm immer zweitrangig, ob man die (mono)funktionale Nutzung seiner Häuser schon von weitem erkennt. Im Gegenteil. »Das nach der Gebäudelehre funktionalisierte Gebäude mit seiner Unterscheidung in verschiedene Gebäudekategorien gibt es ja nur, weil das Haus in seiner Nutzbarkeit nicht so allgemein wie möglich gedacht ist«, führte er einmal aus. Den Unterschied zwischen Bauten für Wohnen und Arbeiten aufzuheben, heißt dann, daß die kommerzielle Bürohausarchitektur etwas hergeben muß, nämlich auf die beherrschende Geste als Firmensitz verzichten. Bei seinem städtebaulichen Projekt Michaelis-Quartier in Hamburg (1995, 1999/2001), ebenfalls ein Ensemble aus Wohnen und Arbeiten und dem städtebaulichen Implantat auf der Theresienhöhe nicht ganz unähnlich, wollte der Bauherr eine tapetenartige Steinfassade hinter einer Glasfront. Das konnte Steidle nicht akzeptieren, weil ihm »das reine und dennoch hohle Repräsentationsgehabe zuwider ist«. Und an anderer Stelle wird er grundsätzlich und führt aus: »Es gibt einfach keinen Anlaß, monumental zu bauen. Einerseits beeindruckt mich Monumentalität nicht sehr, andererseits gestehe ich sie meinen Bauherren auch nicht zu.« Dennoch baut Steidle für Firmen, die nicht gerade dem Kapitalimus fern stehen oder als Globalisierungsgegner alternative Unternehmensstrategien entwickeln.

Strukturelle Harmonie

Für KPMG, gab der Vorstand zu Protokoll, als der Auftrag an Steidle erteilt wurde, war »die Abbildung unserer Unternehmensorganisation in der Gebäudestruktur« ausschlaggebend. Darunter ist zu verstehen, daß das herzhaft gegliederte Haus auf das sich wandelnde Gefüge des Wirtschaftsprüfungs- und Beratungsunternehmens mit Tochterfirmen und assoziierten Partnern für die absehbare Geschäftsentwicklung reagieren kann. Wer sich zu weiterer Interpretation bemüßigt fühlt, mag in den Fassaden, die sich mit den schmalen Fenstern und den nach einer strukturierten Harmonie ordnenden Farben der Pfeiler auch einen Hinweis sehen, daß hier eine Gesellschaft zu Hause ist, die sich logisch und kreativ nach gewissen Regeln im Wirtschaftsleben bewegt, wiederholbare Prozesse, denen immer neue Facetten abgewonnen werden müssen. Der Bauherr, der in anderen Städten bereits in ausgezeichnete Gebäude eingezogen ist (am bekanntesten dürfte dessen Haus von Schneider + Schumacher in Leipzig sein), ließ sich von einer sympathisch profanen Erwartung leiten. Er betrachtet seine Mitarbeiter als »geistig denkende Künstler«, denen man die besten räumlichen Voraussetzungen für ihre Arbeit bieten müsse. Wenn jemand 12 bis 14 Stunden täglich arbeitet, dann ist sein Büro ein Ort, der motivieren und bereits während des produktiven Denkens zur Reproduktion beitragen muß. Andererseits sind die an den Umgang mit Geld gewohnten Investoren so nüchtern, den Quadratmeterpreis pro Arbeitsplatz zu kalkulieren. Diese Parameter führten zu der Entscheidung, die einzelnen Büros so ökonomisch wie möglich (sprich platzsparend) auszulegen, dafür den Gemeinschaftsflächen eine spürbare Erlebnisqualität zu geben: Helligkeit, Raumhöhe, Galerien um ein interessantes Treppenatrium, gesäumt von Teeküchen, gediegenen Besprechungsräumen und einem attraktiven Bistro, ausgestattet mit Kunst und einer aufregenden Lichtinstallation, sollen das gemeinsame Obdach zu einem angenehmen Leistungszentrum machen. Dies traf auch die Weltanschauung der Architekten: »Eine demokratische Gesellschaft findet insbesondere in den allgemein verfügbaren Bereichen ihren Ausdruck«, erklärte Steidle einmal die Sorgfalt, die er beim Wohnungsbau den »unrentablen« Zwischenzonen allgemein verfügbarer Bereiche widmet, weil dort der »Zusammenhang von Ästhetik und Demokratie« erlebbar werde.

Für die Architekten waren die Auflösung und Staffelung der Baumasse um drei Höfe (den Eingangshof an der Ganghoferstraße, den »Bistrohof« gegenüber der alten Messehalle, der den Besuchern des Bistros offen steht, und den »Bibliothekshof« neben dem Lektürepool) eine städtebauliche Entscheidung. Ihnen ging es um Orientierung und Belichtung sowohl der Büros als auch des benachbarten Wohnturms, um Symmetrie und Balance des Baukörpers und eine Korrespondenz mit den gewachsenen Stadtstrukturen. Die Lage des Eingangs resultiert aus der Grundrißentwicklung, lieber wäre es den Architekten gewesen, ihn näher an die U-Bahn-Station zu legen. Aus der Luft gesehen, ordnet sich die Baumasse zu einem behäbigen Gebäudewinkel, aber das wird man als Passant nicht wahrnehmen, da die sieben Geschosse des Hauses nicht mit einer einheitlichen Trauflinie enden, sondern wie bei einem unfertigen Steckspiel (ein Vergleich, den auch das Fassadenskelett aufgibt), das noch weitergebaut werden soll, durch auf allen Seiten »fehlende« Volumen gegliedert

10. Steidle + Partner, KPMG-Gebäude, München, 1995 bis 2002. Entwurfsskizze von Otto Steidle.

10. Steidle + Partner, KPMG building, Munich, 1995 to 2002. Design sketch by Otto Steidle.

interventions. This means that office buildings in cities will have to be more durably planned and built than they have been in the past. And that they have to pay less attention to the uses they have to accommodate and more to their situation in the urban space.« This could be a specific note for the KPMG building, even though durability, prestige and permanence are not key words in Steidle's architectural vocabulary.

Steidle's earliest work was housing, and involved looking for things that could be positively useful to the people they surrounded. It was always of secondary interest to him whether the (single) function of a building could be made out from a distance. On the contrary. »The building that is functionalized according to building theory, with its divisions into various building categories exists only because the building in its usefulness is not thought through as generally as possible«, he once stated. Removing the distinction between buildings for living and working then means that commercial office architecture has to give something up, in other words do without the dominant gesture of being the company head office. In his urban project for the Michaelis-Quartier in Hamburg (1995, 1999/2001), also an offices and housing ensemble, and not dissimilar to the urban implant on the Theresienhöhe, the client wanted a wallpaper-like stone façade behind a glass wall. Steidle could not accept that, because »mere and therefore hollow and pompous behaviour about prestige [is] repugnant« to him. And elsewhere he gets down to basics and says: »There is simply no reason for building monumentally. On the one hand I am not very impressed by monumental qualities, and on the other hand I am not going to concede my client the right to have it.« Even so, Steidle builds for firms that are not exactly all that far away from capitalism or developing alternative business strategies as opponents of globalization.

Structural harmony

The KPMG board pointed out when the commission was given to Steidle that the key thing was »illustrating our company organization in the structure of the building«. This means that the substantially structured building can respond to the changing structure of this accountant and consultant practice with subsidiary companies and associated partners to accommodate anticipated commercial developments. Anyone who feels obliged to provide further interpretations may also see the façades and the colours of the piers, bringing a sense of order and harmony, along with the narrow windows, as in indication that this is the home of a company that moves logically and creatively in the financial world according to certain rules, repeatable processes from which new facets constantly have to be gained. The client, who has already moved into some excellent buildings in other cities (the best-known must be its building by Schneider + Schumacher in Leipzig), allowed itself to be guided by an attractively mundane set of expectations. It sees its employees as »intellectually thinking artists«, who have to be provided with the best possible spatial conditions for their work. If someone works 12 to 14 hours a day, then his or her office is a place that has to motivate and make a contribution to reproduction even while productive thought is taking place. On the other hand the developers, who are used to handling money, are calm and collected enough to calculate the price of each workspace by the square metre. These parameters led to the decision that the individual offices should be laid out as economically as possible (for which read: to save as much space as possible), but to compensate by giving the communal areas a discernible sense of quality experience: light, height, galleries placed around an interesting staircase atrium, fringed by small kitchens, solid conference rooms and an attractive bistro, furnished with art and a exciting light installation – all these are intended to make this shared shelter into a pleasant achievement centre. This also fitted in with the architects' philosophy: »A democratic society finds its expression especially in areas that are generally available«, was Steidle's explanation for the care he devoted to the »unprofitable« intermediate zones of generally available areas when building homes, because that is where one can experience »co-operation between aesthetics and democracy«.

For the architects, breaking the building mass down and staggering it around three courtyards (the entrance courtyard in Ganghoferstraße, the »bistro courtyard« opposite the old exhibition hall, which is available to bistro users, and the »library courtyard« by the reading area) was an urban development decision. They were concerned with the orientation and lighting of the offices and the neighbouring high-rise flats as well, with

dert ist. Also war der Städtebau wirklich wichtiger als die spekulative Bereichsaufteilung nach den sich wandelnden Geschäftsfeldern in einer unsicheren Weltwirtschaft. Aber: beides scheint zusammenzupassen oder läßt sich anspruchslos verändern. Zum Beispiel hat sich das Unternehmen inzwischen von einer Tochterfirma getrennt. Nun muß zwischen den Wirtschaftsprüfern und den Consultants im obersten Geschoß eine gläserne Trennscheibe auf der Treppe die formale Ordnung wiederherstellen. Hatte Steidle doch vorhergesagt, als er in anderem Zusammenhang auf den Ausgleich zwischen Struktur und Form einging: »Insofern glaube ich, daß dem erinnerbaren Haus ein strukturelles Prinzip innewohnen kann, und daß es dem Leben relativ leicht fällt, sich darin einzunisten.«

Tragwerk und Haustechnik

Konstruktiv besteht das Gebäude aus einem Stahlbetonskelett mit Flachdecken. Runde Stützen, wo keine Wandanschlüsse nötig sind, tragen entlang des Treppenatriums die Lasten ab, von dort spannen die Decken zu schlanken, kantigen Stützen im gängigen Büroraster von 1.35 m an der Fassade. Hier lassen sich problemlos Gipskarton-Trennwände anschließen, um Bürozellen über zwei, drei oder auch mehrere Achsen abzutrennen. Zu den Fluren sind die Arbeitsplätze raumhoch verglast. Statt einer Klimaanlage hat man sich für ökologischere (was den Energieverbrauch angeht) und für die Mitarbeiter komfortablere thermisch aktivierte Betondecken entschieden. Dabei wird durch eingelegte Rohre über einen Wasserkreislauf die schwere Masse zur Stabilisierung der Raumtemperatur genutzt. Die Behaglichkeit wird vor allem dadurch hergestellt, daß diese Konstruktion dem alten Grundsatz der Gebäudephysiologie, die Temperatur von Raum und Umgebungsflächen möglichst anzugleichen, gerecht wird. Zur Verbesserung der Akustik sind stellenweise gelochte Gipskartonplatten unter die Betondecken gehängt. Beim Bau ist allerdings ein erhöhter Planungsaufwand erforderlich, da Änderungen nachträglich nur mit unverhältnismäßigem Aufwand möglich sind. Die Installation muß außerdem auf die verborgenen Rohrharfen abgestimmt werden. Das betraf zum Beispiel die runden, flachen Deckenleuchten in den Verkehrsbereichen, deren Position vor dem Betonieren eindeutig bestimmt war. In den Büros, die mit einem Doppelboden ausgerüstet sind, hat man den vorgesehenen Lichtauslaß nicht mehr genutzt und statt dessen mobile Deckenfluter verteilt. Unter den Fenstern sind unscheinbare Radiatoren montiert, die große Halle wird durch eine zusätzliche Lüftungsanlage konditioniert. Die erforderlichen Geräte sind in den Installationskernen zwischen den Teeküchen der Kombi-Zonen verborgen.

Eine Kunsthalle

Blickfang und Mittelpunkt des zweibündig angelegten Büromäanders ist eine über alle Geschosse reichende Treppe. Zu ihr orientieren sich die zu Galerien ausgebildeten Flure. Die unteren beiden Ebenen sind als Foyer durch doppelt hohe Stützen zusammengefaßt. Unter Architekten heißt so eine geradlinige, schier endlose Stiege »Himmelstreppe«. Gottfried Böhm hat sie vor zehn Jahren beim Amtsgericht in Kerpen gebaut, Richard Meier zuletzt bei der Siemens-Hauptverwaltung in München. So ein Aufstieg ist beflügelnd, er kann einem Unternehmen die stufenweise nach oben weisende Wachstumskurve bedeuten, den Angestellten beim täglichen Auf und Ab an seine mögliche Karriere erinnern. Der Nachteil ist, daß sich bei solchen »einfältigen« Raumkunstwerken mit jeder Ebene der ideale Antritt immer weiter von der Mitte entfernt. Aus diesem Grund haben die Architekten jeweils zwei Geschosse mit einem weiteren Treppenlauf verbunden. Die Stufen bestehen aus geöltem Eichenholz, die Wangen aus lackierten Stahlblechen, die nicht sonderlich sorgfältig behandelt sind. Aber das war den Architekten nicht so wichtig. Sie wollten die Materialität des schweren Stahls erkennen lassen. Aus solchen Platten werden Schiffsrümpfe geschweißt, da muß man das zur Form geronnene Erz noch ahnen – sonst könnte es sich ja auch ebenso um lackiertes Holz oder Gipskarton handeln.

Ein Novum sind die umlaufenden Glasbrüstungen. Das trauten sich die Architekten – die sonst eher mit Stäben und Blechen »greifbare« Geländer bauen –, weil die spiegelnde Transparenz mit dem Lichtkunstwerk von Ingo Maurer zusammenhängt. Maurer hat die Zackenlinie der Stufenunterseite an den Kanten mit farbigen Leuchtstoffröhren nachgezeichnet. Einfach, manchmal zweifach und sich überschneidend glühen die farbigen Konturen unter dem schwarzen Treppenbalken. In den gläsernen Brüstungen und den dahinter liegenden Bürotrennwänden vervielfachen sich die Lichtspuren. Aber von außen erkennt man nicht sofort, ob man die Quelle sieht oder eine der flirrenden Widerspiegelungen. Auch das ließe sich metaphorisch auf das bisweilen trügerische Geschäftsleben übertragen, vielleicht zur Warnung, wenn man sich an die aktuellen Zusammenbrüche amerikanischer Gesellschaften erinnert. Über dem Treppenkunstwerk öffnet sich das Gebäude. Allerdings wird der weiß-blaue Himmel über München nicht ungeniert hereingelassen. Ein verstellbares Lamellendach aus roten Glaspaneelen taucht die Halle in feurige Glut, sie leckt sich über die runden Stützentrommeln, bricht sich auf den Wänden, dringt in die Bürozellen und wird dort vom dunklen Nadelfilz oder von den schwarzen Basaltina-Platten am Hallenboden verschluckt.

Arbeitsplätze

Die Ausstattung der Büros ist einfach. Eine gelochte Buchenholztafel hinter der Tür dient der Schallabsorption, verbirgt die Installationen, nimmt Schalter auf und bietet ein paar Kleiderhaken an. Alternativ hätte man die Stahlprofile der Glastrennwände mit sondergefertigten Paneelen ausrüsten müssen. Die Ökonomie hatte an unwichtigen Positionen eben Vorrang. In der Höhe geteilte Jalousien regulieren den Einblick und reflektieren das Licht an die Decke. Die dunkel gebeizten Büroschränke, die sich in niedriger Ausführung auch in den Kombi-Zonen finden, sind sehr tief. Da wünschte man sich eine »architektonischere« Lösung, Regale und Container, die mit den Raumkonturen harmonieren.

Um so sorgfältiger wurde der Konferenzbereich inszeniert. Schon die Namen der Kompartimente Moscow, Sydney, Casablanca … – Städte, in denen das Unternehmen KPMG eigene Niederlassungen besitzt – suggerieren weltläufige Eleganz. Die technische Aus-

symmetry and balance within the body of the building and a correspondence with mature urban structures. The position of the entrance is the result of the way the ground plan developed, the architects would have preferred to place it nearer the underground station. Seen from the air, the mass of the building forms an orderly and solid angular structure, but it is not possible to see that as a passer-by, as the building's seven storeys do not end in a uniform eaves line, but as if they are part of an unfinished construction game (a comparison that applies to the façade skeleton as well) that will see further building work, articulated on all sides by »missing« volumes. So urban development really was more important than speculative division into areas according to changing business fields within an uncertain global economy. But: both seem to fit together or can be changed quite simply. For example, the firm has recently parted company with one of its subsidiaries. Now formal order has to be restored between the accountants and the consultants on the top floor by a glazed partition on the staircase. And in fact Steidle had prophesied when going into the balance between structure and form in another context: »To that extent I believe that a memorable building can have a structural principle inherent in it, and that it is relatively easier for life to settle down in there.«

Load-bearing structure and services

Structurally speaking, the building consists of a reinforced concrete skeleton with flat slabs. Where no wall connections are needed, round supports distribute the load along the staircase atrium, and from there the floors are attached to slender, angular supports on the usual office grid pattern of 1.35 m by the façade. Here it is possible to attach plasterboard partitions without difficulty, to produce office cells over two, three or even several axes. The workplaces are glazed room-high on the corridor side. Instead of air-conditioning, a decision was made in favour of thermally active concrete ceilings, which are more ecologically sound (as far as energy consumption is concerned) and more comfortable for the employees. Here the heavy mass is used to stabilize the room temperature by means of inserted piping with water circulating in it. The comfort derives above all from the fact that this structure does justice to the old building physiology maxim of matching the temperature of the room and the surrounding surfaces to as great an extent as possible. Perforated plasterboard sheets are suspended under the concrete ceilings in place to improve the acoustics. However, a great deal of attention has to be paid to planning at the building stage, as subsequent changes are possible only with a disproportionate amount of effort and expense. The installation also has to be matched to the concealed chorded cooling tubes. For example, this affected the round, flat ceiling lights in the circulation areas whose position was clearly fixed before the concrete was poured. In the offices, which are equipped with a double floor, a decision was made not to use the planned light outlet, opting instead for mobile ceiling floods. Inconspicuous radiators are mounted under the windows, and the large hall has an additional ventilation plant. The necessary equipment is concealed in the service cores between the small kitchens in the combi-zones.

An art gallery

The eye-catching feature and centre of the meandering rows of offices on either side of the corridors is a staircase rising through all floors. The corridors become galleries at this point and face the staircase. The two lower levels are brought together to form a foyer by the use of double-height supports. Architects call a straight, well-nigh endless staircase like this a »Jacob's ladder«. Gottfried Böhm used one ten years ago for the district court in Kerpen, and Richard Meier most recently in the Siemens headquarters in Munich. A staircase like this is inspiring, it can suggest a growth curve that is rising step by step to a company, and remind employees of their careers as they go up and down each day. The disadvantage is that with such »artless« three-dimensional works of art the ideal access point becomes increasingly far from the centre with every level. For this reason the architects have connected each pair of two storeys with another flight of stairs. The individual steps are made of oiled oak and the stringers of painted steel sheets that are not treated particularly carefully. But that was not so important to the architects. They wanted the material quality of the heavy steel to be visible. Ships' hulls are welded from steel sheets of this kind, and you should have a sense of the ore running into the mould – otherwise you could just as well have painted wood or plasterboard.

The continuous glass parapets are a novel feature. The architects permitted themselves this touch – otherwise they tend to build banisters that can be »grasped« using rods and sheet metal – because the reflecting transparency links up with Ingo Maurer's light artwork. Maurer has picked out the edges of the serrated line of the underside of the steps with coloured fluorescent tubes. The coloured outlines glow singly, two-fold and sometimes overlapping under the black beams of the stairs. The traces of light are multiplied in the glass parapets and the office partitions behind them. But from the outside it is not possible to make out straight away whether you are looking at the source or one of the flickering reflections. This too could be applied metaphorically to the fact that there are sometimes deceptions in commercial life, perhaps as a warning, if one remembers the current collapse of American corporations. The building opens up above the staircase artwork. But the white-blue sky above Munich is not admitted casually. An adjustable slatted roof made up of red glass panels plunges the hall into a fiery glow, licking over the coloured support drums, breaking against the walls, penetrating the office cells and swallowed up there by the dark needled felt or the black Basaltina slabs.

Workplaces

The offices are simply furnished. A perforated beechwood panel behind the door absorbs sound, conceals the service ducts, accommodates switches and provides a few clothes-pegs. Otherwise it would have been necessary to equip the steel profiles of the glass partitions with specially made panels. Economy was made the main concern at unimportant points. Vertically divided blinds stop people looking in from the outside and reflect light on to the ceiling. The dark-stained office cupboards, which are also to be found in the combi-

rüstung dieser Besprechungs- und Speiseräume verbirgt sich im Mobiliar, auch hier wieder helles Buchenholz für Tische und Schränke. Ingo Maurer hat flache Alu-Lichtsegel unter die Decken gehängt, aus deren weichen Falten individuell eingestellte Halogenleuchten strahlen. Auch die Flure im Konferenzbereich sind großzügig und weit. Man kann sich vorstellen, wie vor den aufwendig gedämmten, zum Teil doppelt angeordneten Türen die Geschäftspartner an den Kunstwerken entlangflanieren und die Diversifizierung ihrer Unternehmen in neue Märkte erörtern. Warum sollte sich Arbeit nicht mit einem kulturellen Ambiente verbinden lassen?

Ein besonderer Ort ist das gemeinsam mit Ingo Maurer geplante elegante Bistro. Hier treffen sich Sparsamkeit und Ordnung, Farbe und Licht. Die normale Raumhöhe der Büros wird scheinbar aufgehoben durch eine glänzende, schwarz gestrichene Decke, die den Raum höher erscheinen läßt, als er tatsächlich ist. Die grauen, roten und weißen Tische sind reduziert auf Platten und Wangen an den Stirnseiten, als handele es sich um eine simple geometrische Papierfaltung. Davor stehen schwarze Holzstühle, eine ausgeschäumte Konstruktion, die nur 200 Gramm wiegt. Die Lampen pendeln an dünnen Kabeln, die sich wie eine Gardinenschnur mit einer Schlaufe in der Höhe verstellen lassen. Ein lose liegender Ring schützt vor der Blendung der nackten Glühlampen.

Fenster, das Lob der Wand

Als sei der Angestellte die Hauptsache des Unternehmens, bildet sich das schmale, raumhohe Fenster, das den einzelnen Arbeitsplatz bestimmt, nach außen ab. Sein schlankes Format ist Steidles private Ambition. Er beruft sich auf die Sentenz von Rainer Maria Rilke, mit beiden Händen das Fenster zu öffnen, um den Morgen zu begrüßen. Dieser interpretierbare Modul des Unternehmens bestimmt vielhundertfach die Fassade. Außer im Erdgeschoß mit den Konferenzräumen, deren zweiachsige Öffnungen zusätzlich von einer dritten Scheibe geschützt sind, marschieren die schmalhohen Öffnungsschlitze in allen Geschossen wie ein endloses Stakkato um das Haus. Die Schauseite liegt natürlich an der Ganghoferstraße, wo sie den Eingangshof einbeziehen (der noch auf eine 8 m hohe Skulptur von Olafur Eliasson wartet).

Sie besteht aus der bereits im Wettbewerb erwähnten, mit keramischen Platten verkleideten Fassade. Die Gebäudeflanken und rückwärtigen Außenwände sind farbig geputzt. Die farbliche Gestaltung, die nach einem mathematischen Kalkül geordnet scheint, stammt von Erich Wiesner, Steidles langjährigem Partner bei solchen Aufgaben. Um den rätselhaften semantischen Code zu entschlüsseln, der dann doch keine geheime Botschaft enthält (wie die farbigen Knotenschnüre der Inkas), muß man sich partienweise mit dem Haus verständigen. Am besten beim mehrfachen Entlangspazieren an der Front. Ob sich den Mitarbeitern die Verteilung des Farbspektrums schon richtig eingeprägt hat?

Zunächst verbinden sich die beiden unteren Geschosse durch zwei dunkle Grüntöne mit der Erde. Darüber folgt ein dreifaches, noch grün durchwirktes Orange, dem sich – der Sonne nun schon verdächtig nahe – ein helles Gelb dazugesellt (bei den zurückspringenden Flächen sogar Weiß). Während die senkrechten Pfeiler sozusagen den Grundakkord vorgeben, antworten die waagrechten Deckenbrüstungen kontrapunktisch. Auch die Fensterprofile folgen dieser Räson. So kreuzen sich zwei Farbbewegungen als räumliche Streifen. Damit aber nicht genug. Auch die Fläche kommt zu ihrem Recht. Jeder zweite Pfeiler hat eine hellgraue Seite, die neben den spiegelnden Scheiben verschluckt wird. So erlebt man beim Hingehen einmal die farbigen, schmalen Fenster, auf dem Rückweg scheinbar doppelt breite Öffnungen. Als hätte jemand ruckartig eine Riesen-Jalousie verstellt, um die hinter den Dingen liegenden Wirklichkeit zu zeigen. Man mag das wieder als einen Hinweis auf das janusköpfige Unternehmen lesen: zu beraten und zu prüfen. Da diese an den Kanten auf Gehrung geformten Keramikplatten vor die tragenden Fassadenpfeiler gesetzt sind, tauchen sie an den Außenkanten zweifach auf; an den einspringenden Kanten fehlt jeweils ein Keramikelement, hier stoßen die Fensterprofile direkt aneinander. So kann der Rhythmus des Betonskeletts ungestört bleiben. Ein Vorteil der gebrannten Platten liegt auch darin, daß sie keine zusätzliche Blechverwahrung brauchen. Dadurch waren die schlanken Leibungen möglich.

Streetlife

Liegt die Sensation des Hauses jetzt außen oder innen? Wir kehren dahin zurück, wo unsere Exkursion begonnen hat. Im Café »Westend« lassen wir die Fassade zur Ruhe kommen, verhalten uns still und merken uns das Bild der Farben. Noch brennt in den Büros überall Licht, das mit zunehmender Dunkelheit die Fassade verschwinden läßt. Erst spät verlöschen die Lampen bis auf ein paar sparsame Lebenszeichen, die das Haus in die Nacht begleiten und seine Transparenz erhalten. Dafür füllt sich das Lokal, der behäbige alte Block aus den späten zwanziger Jahren kann das aushalten, Menschen, Musik, laute Gespräche und Bier nicht zu knapp. Morgen früh, wenn hier der kalte Rauch über den hochgestellten Stühlen liegt, werden sich die Verhältnisse wieder umkehren und die farbigen Bänder der Fassaden auf der anderen Straßenseite als heiteres Pasticcio die Angestellten begrüßen. »In München und Oberbayern ... zelebriert man in der Architektur zuerst die Lebensfreude: ›Mir san mir‹, heißt es. Das macht ... weniger anfällig, aber auch weniger offen für das Neue«, hat Otto Steidle die ihm mitgegebene Mentalität erklärt. »Hier ist es weniger der Stil, der ausgekostet wird, sondern die Tradition der Vernunft und der Praktikabilität.« Insofern ergänzen sich die beiden Straßenseiten kongenial und schreiben einen Stadtteil lebendig fort.

Übrigens wurde im April 2002 eine Straße des Quartiers nach August Kühn benannt. Zeit zum Aufstehn. Jetzt lohnt es sich.

11. Olafur Eliasson, Skulptur für den Eingangshof des KPMG-Gebäudes in München.

11. Olafur Eliasson, sculpture for the entrance courtyard of the KPMG building in Munich.

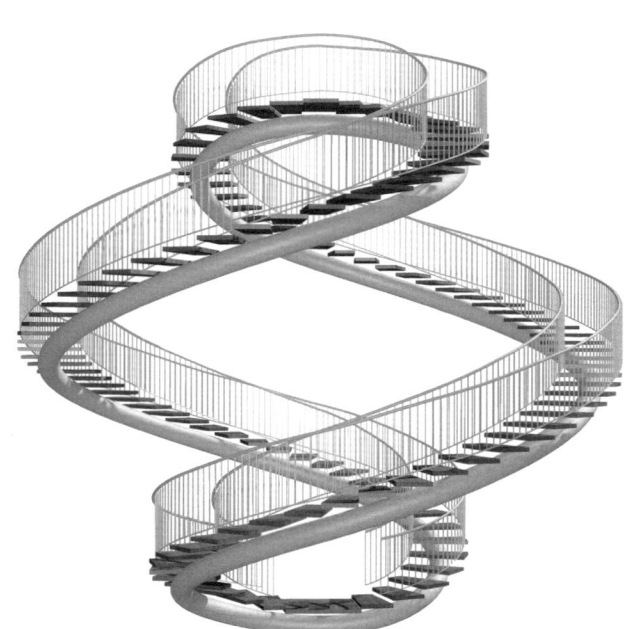

zones in a lower version, are very deep. A more »architectural« solution was being sought here, shelves and containers that harmonize with the lines of the room.

The conference area was staged all the more carefully. The very names of the meeting rooms, Moscow, Sydney, Casablanca ... – cities in which KPMG has its own branches – suggest worldly elegance. The technical equipment in these conference- and dining-rooms is concealed in the furniture, and here too light beechwood is used for tables and cupboards. Ingo Maurer has suspended shallow aluminium light awnings under the ceilings, with individually adjusted halogen lamps shining out of their soft folds. The corridors in the conference area are also generous and wide. It is possible to imagine the business partners strolling up and down past the works of art in front of the elaborately insulated doors, some of which are double, discussing their companies' diversification into new markets. Why should work not be combined with a cultural ambience?

The elegant bistro, planned jointly with Ingo Maurer, is a special place. Here frugality and order, colour and light meet. The normal height of the offices seems to be cancelled out by a shining, black painted ceiling that makes the room seem higher than it actually is. The grey, red and white tables are reduced to tops and outside pieces, as though we are dealing with a simple matter of geometrical paper folding. In front of them are black wooden chairs, a foam construction weighing only 200 grams. The lamps swing on thin cables that can be adjusted in terms of height like a curtain cord with a loop. A loose ring protects from dazzle by naked bulbs.

Window, praising the wall

To give the impression that the employee is the main thing in the company, the narrow, room-high window that defines each individual workplace tapers towards the outside. The slender format is Steidle's private ambition. He quotes Rainer Maria Rilke's statement that one should open the window with both hands to greet the morning. This company module, which is open to interpretation, determines the façade many hundreds of times. With the exception of the ground floor with the conference rooms, where the double-axis apertures are additionally protected by a third pane, the narrow vertical slits march all round the building on all floors, like an infinite staccato. Of course the show side is in Ganghoferstraße, where it includes the entrance courtyard (which is still waiting for an 8-m high sculpture by Olafur Eliasson).

This side consists of the façade clad with ceramic tiles that has already been mentioned in the competition. The flanks of the building and the outside walls at the back are rendered in colour. The colour design, which seems to be based on mathematical calculations, is by Erich Wiesner, who has been Steidle's partner in such projects for years. To decipher the mysterious semantic code, which then turns out not to carry any secret message (like the Incas' knotted coloured cords), it is necessary to understand the building section by section. This is best done by walking up and down the façade several times. Have the employees learned correctly how the colour spectrum is distributed yet?

First of all, the bottom two stories are linked to the ground by two dark shades of green. Above this is a three-fold orange, still worked through with green, and this is then joined – already suspiciously close to the sun – by a light yellow (in fact white in recessed areas). While the vertical piers sound the basic chord, as it were, the horizontal floor parapets respond contrapuntally. The window bars also follow this reasoning. So two colour movements cross in the form of three-dimensional stripes. But that is not all. Flat surfaces come into their own as well. Every second pier has a light grey side that is swallowed up alongside the reflecting panes. Thus when approaching the building you experience the coloured, narrow windows, and on the way back the apertures seem to be doubly wide. As though someone had suddenly adjusted a gigantic blind to show the reality that lies behind things. This can be read as another reference to this Janus-faced company: advising and auditing. As these ceramic tiles, which were designed for mitre-joints, are placed in front of the load-bearing façade piers, they appear twice on the outside edges; one ceramic element is missing at the recessed edges, here the window bars meet directly. This means that the rhythm of the concrete skeleton can remain undisturbed. One advantage of the fired tiles is that they do not need any additional metal flashing. This made the slender reveals possible.

Streetlife

And so is the sensational aspect of the building inside or outside? Let us go back to where we started. In the »Westend« café we allow the façade to come to rest, sit quietly and notice the image created by the colours. There are still lights in the offices everywhere, making the façade disappear as darkness falls. The lights do not go off until late, leaving just a few signs of life that accompany the building into the night and maintain its transparent quality. But the café fills up, the solid old late twenties block can take it, people, music, loud conversations and no shortage of beer. Tomorrow morning, when the stale smoke is still around the chairs on the tables here, the circumstances will change again and the coloured bands on the façades on the other side of the road will greet the employees like a cheerful pastiche. »In Munich and Upper Bavaria ... joie de vivre is the first thing to be celebrated in architecture: »We are what we are« is what we say. This makes us less delicate, but also less open to new things«, is how Otto Steidle interprets the mentality he has inherited. »Here we are less likely to savour style, but to choose the traditions of reason and practicability.« In this respect the two sides of the road complement each other perfectly and represent a lively continuation of this part of the city.

Incidentally, a street in the quarter was named after August Kühn in April 2002. Time to get up. It's worth it now.

1. Luftaufnahme. (Photo: Reinhard Görner.)
2. Lageplan.

1. Aerial view. (Photo: Reinhard Görner.)
2. Site plan.

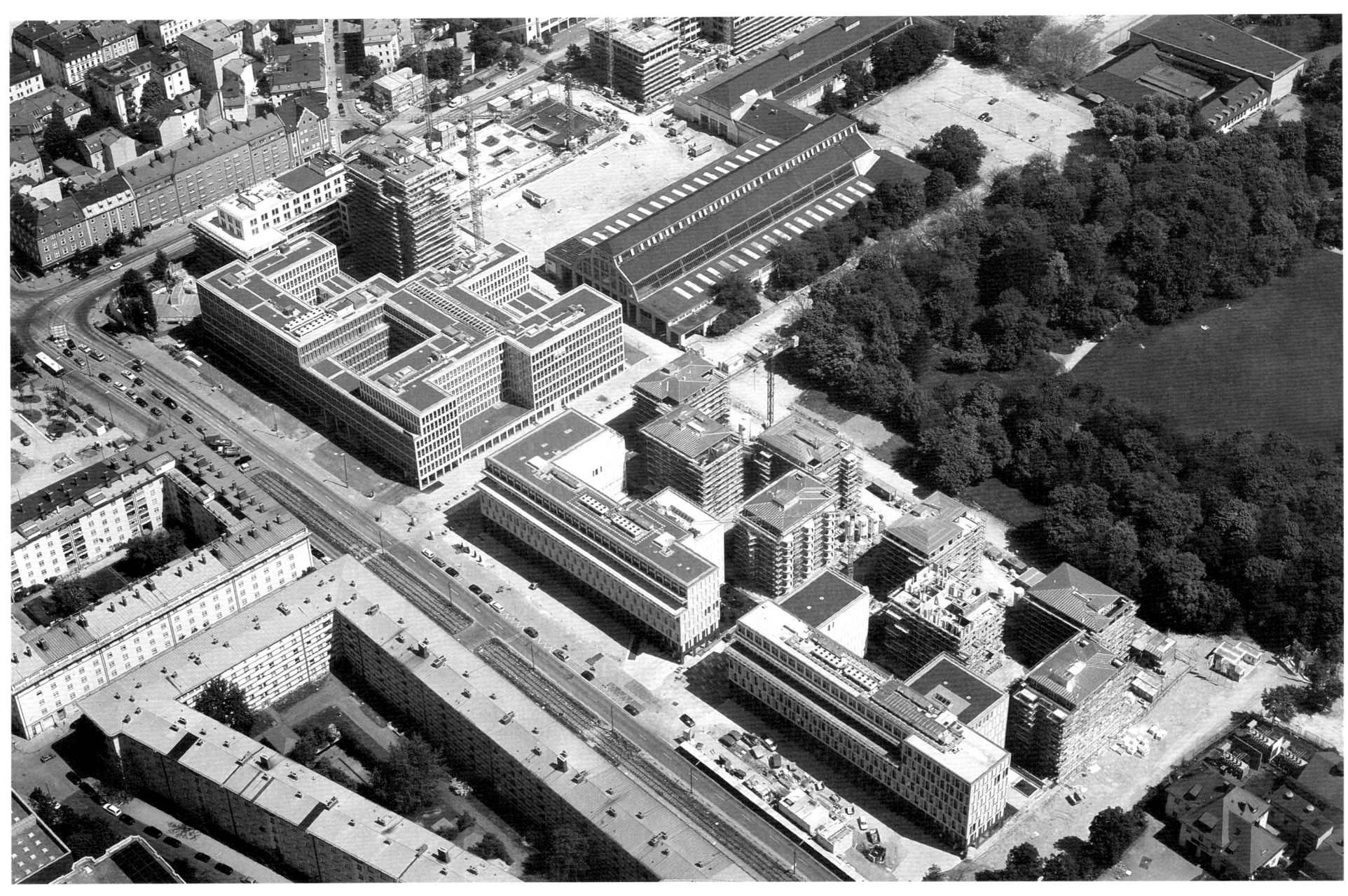

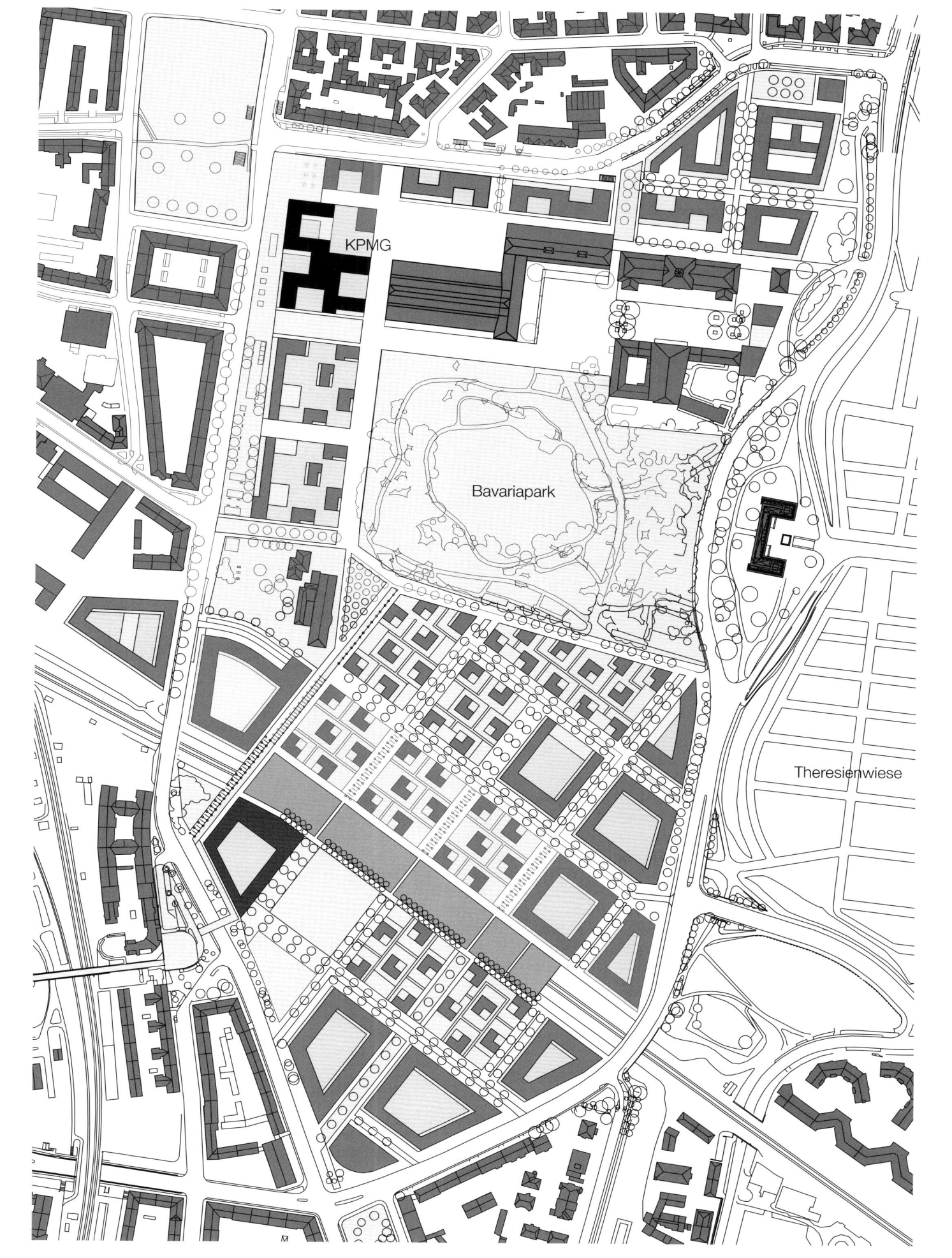

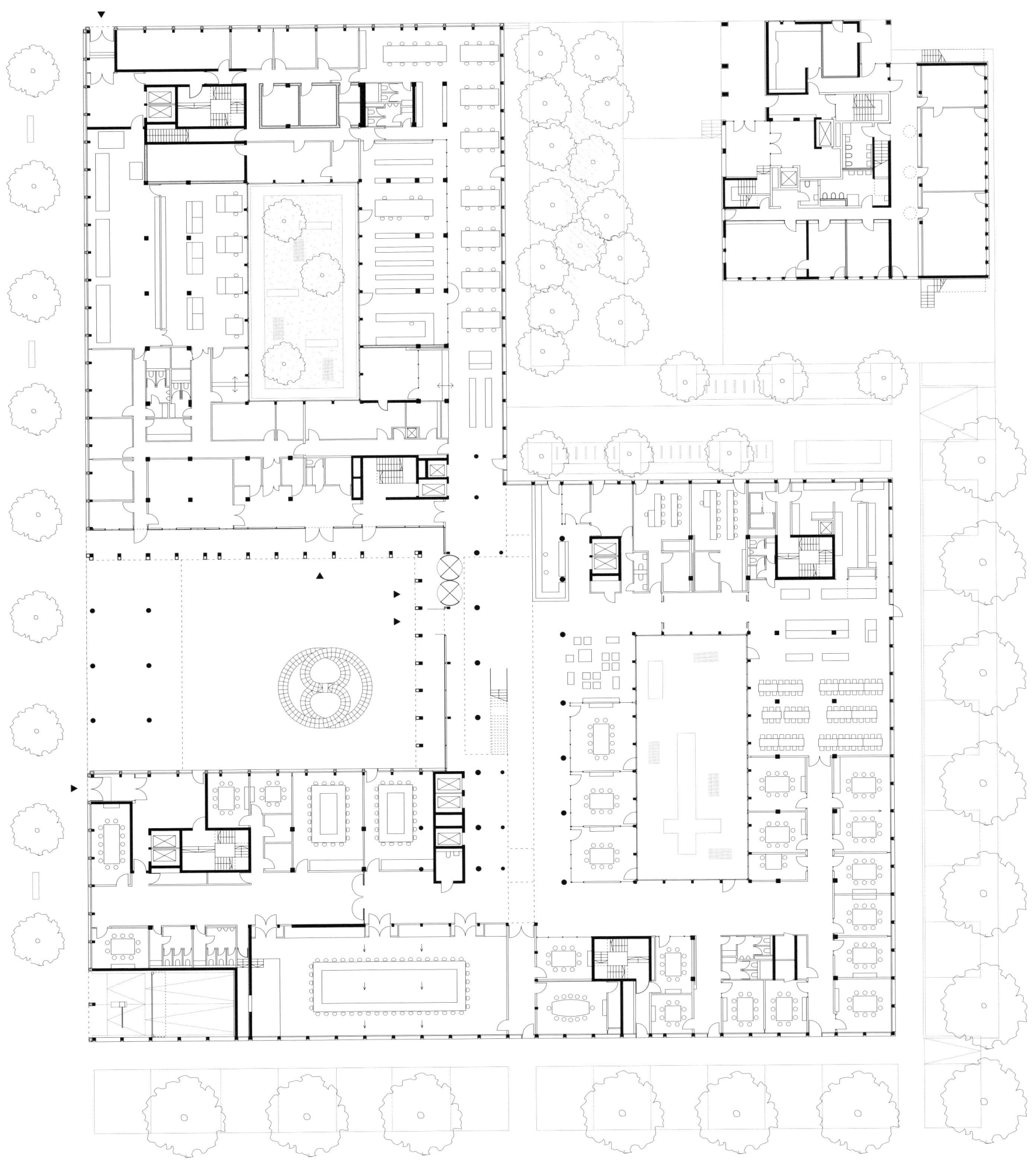

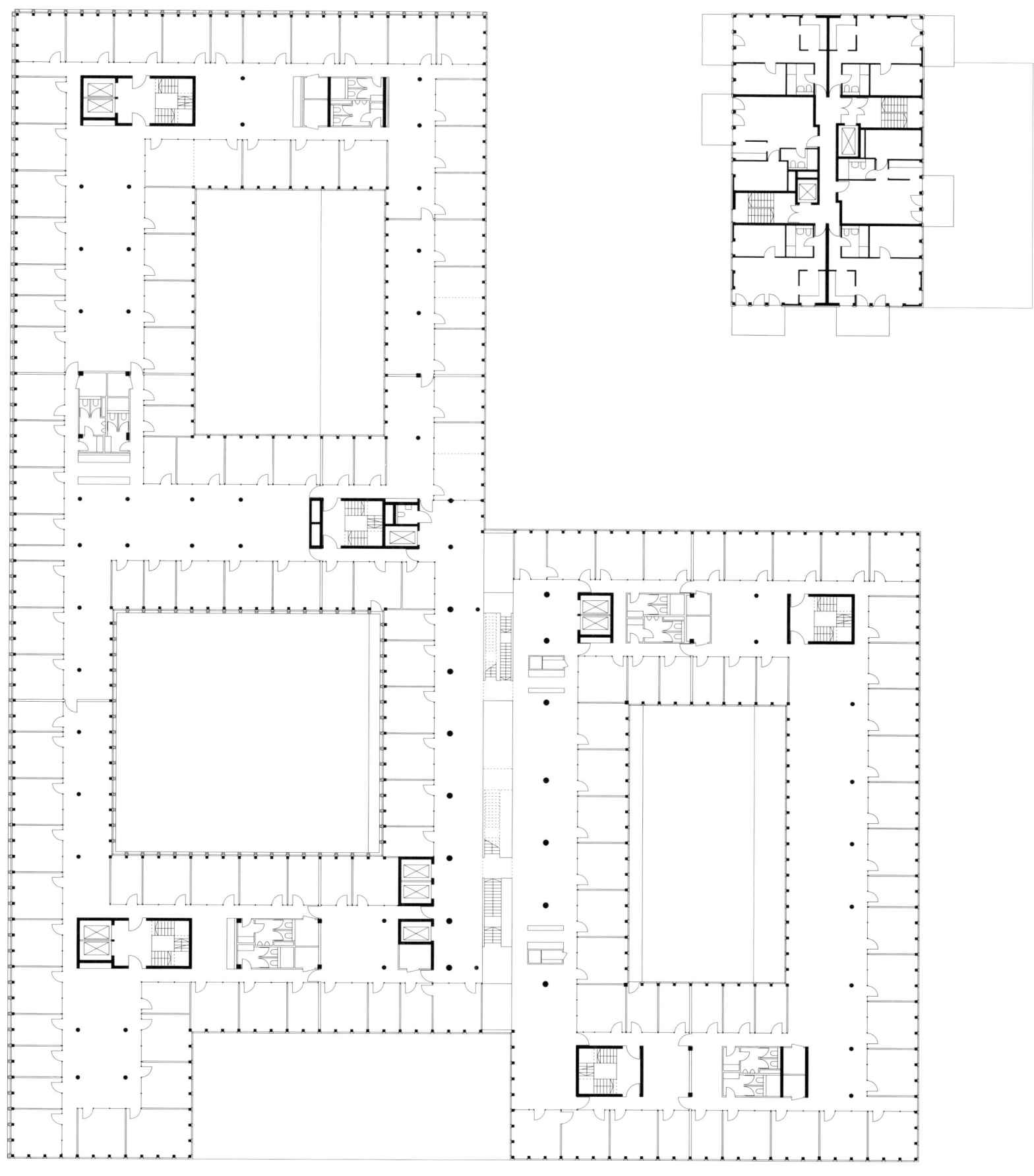

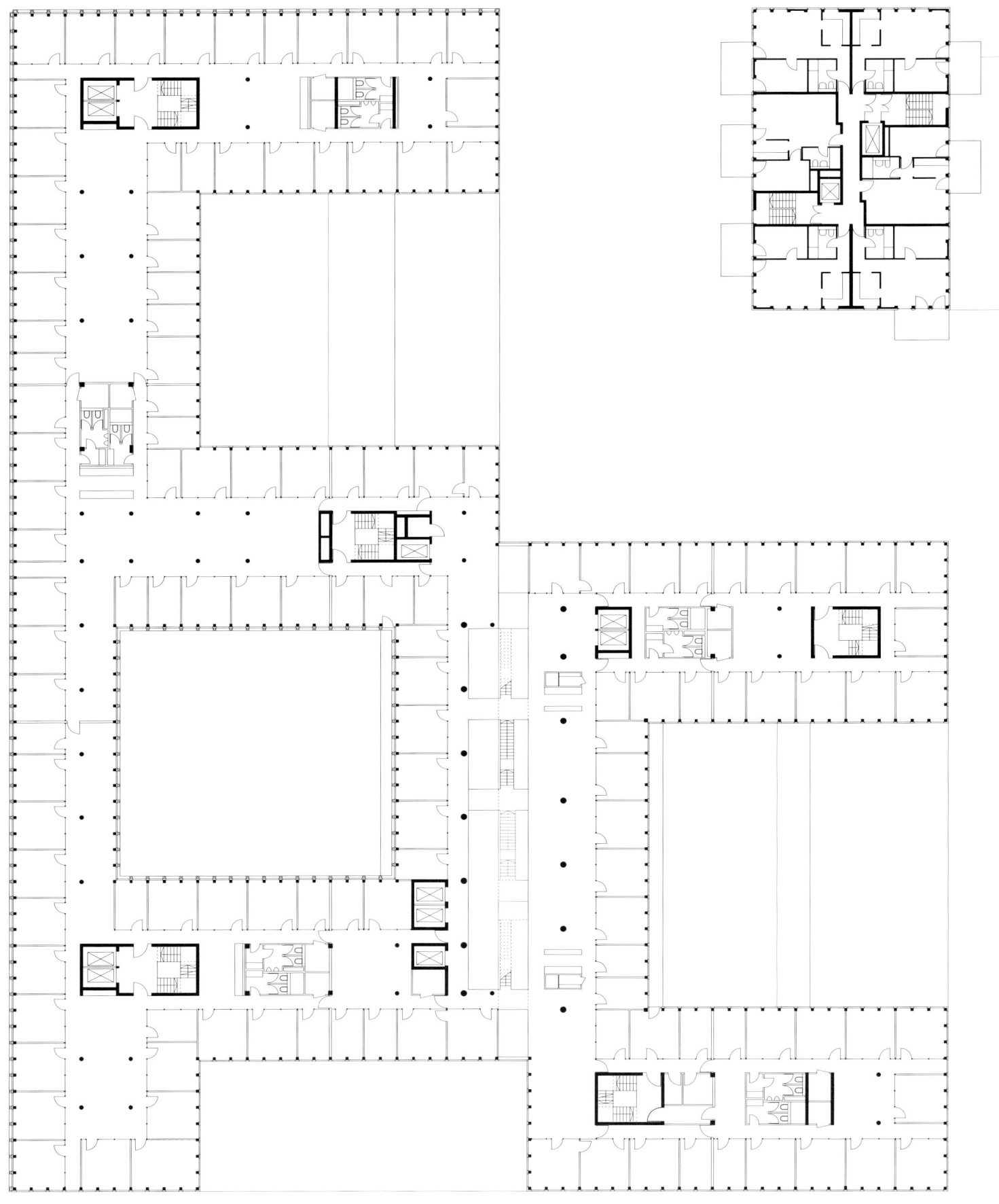

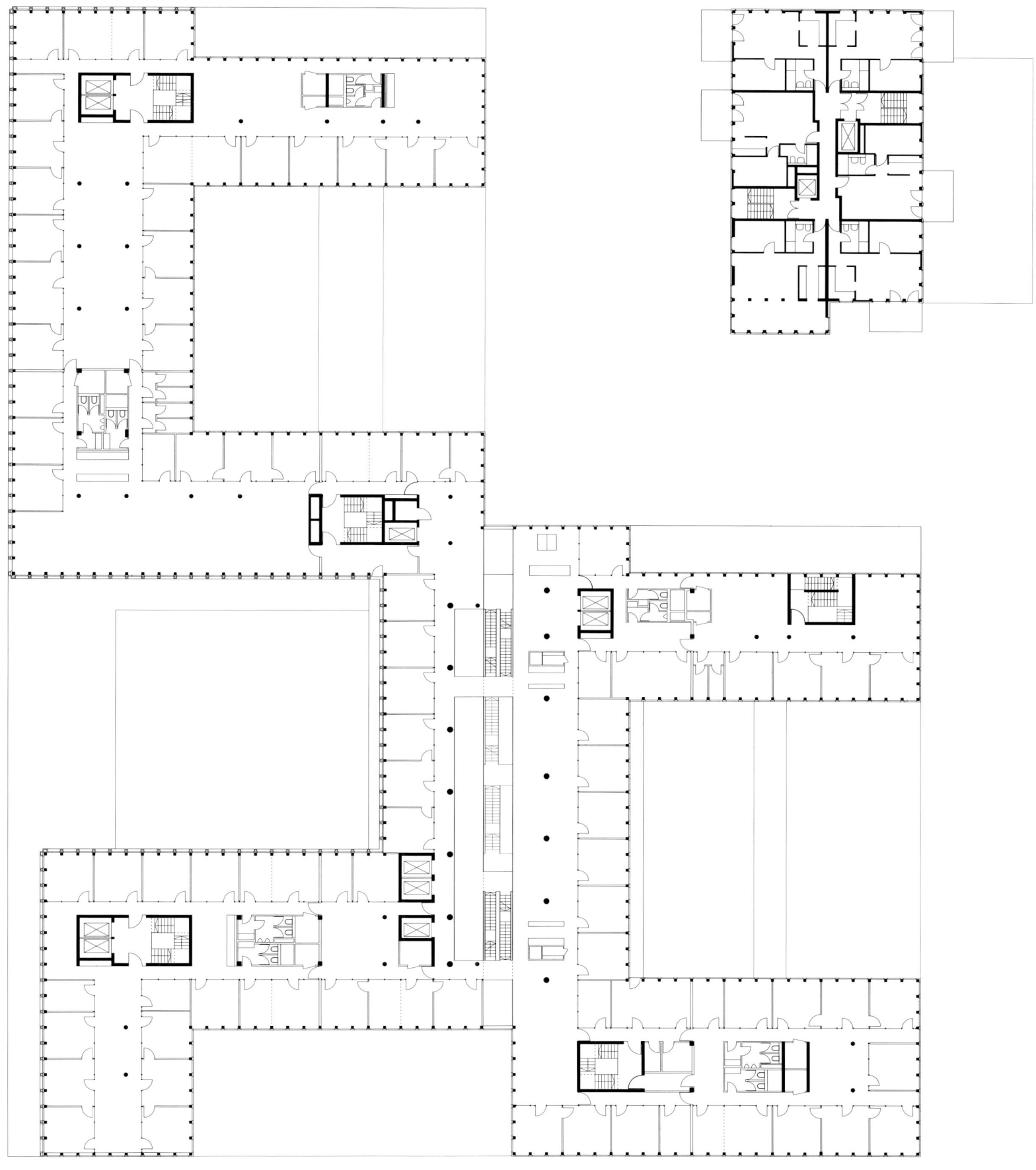

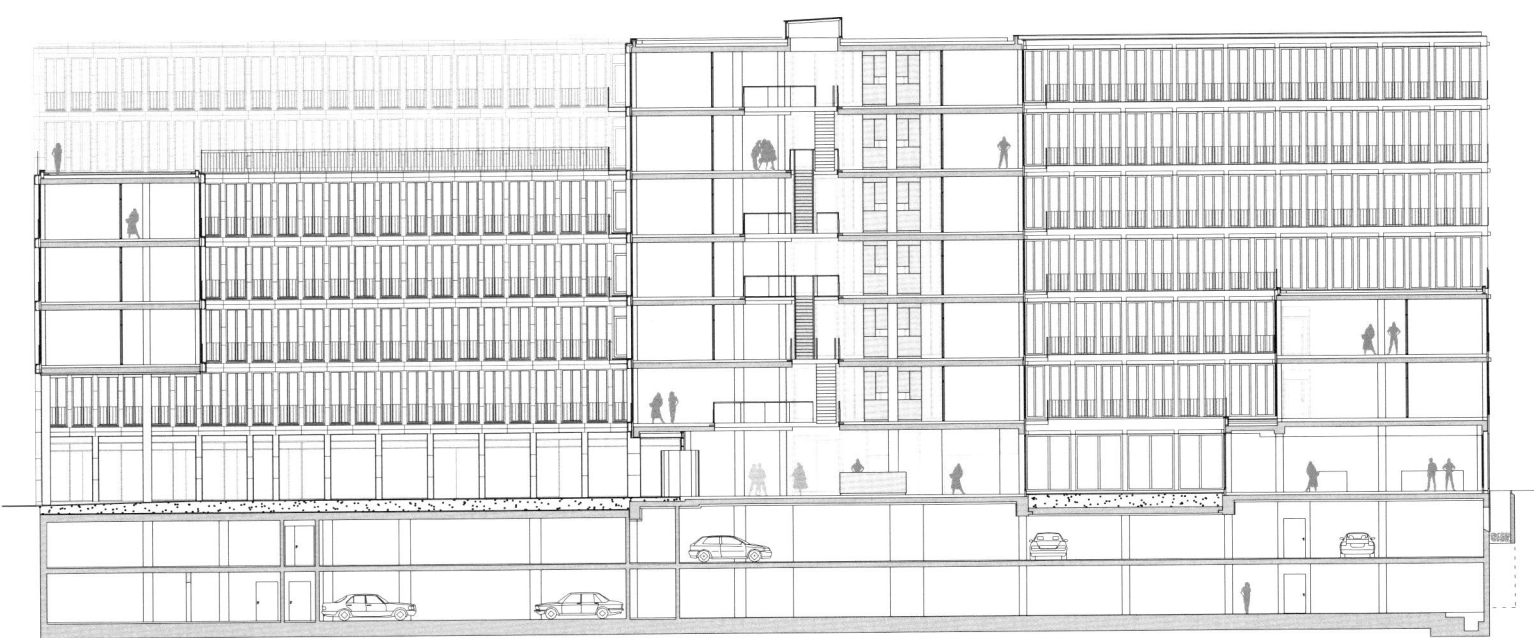
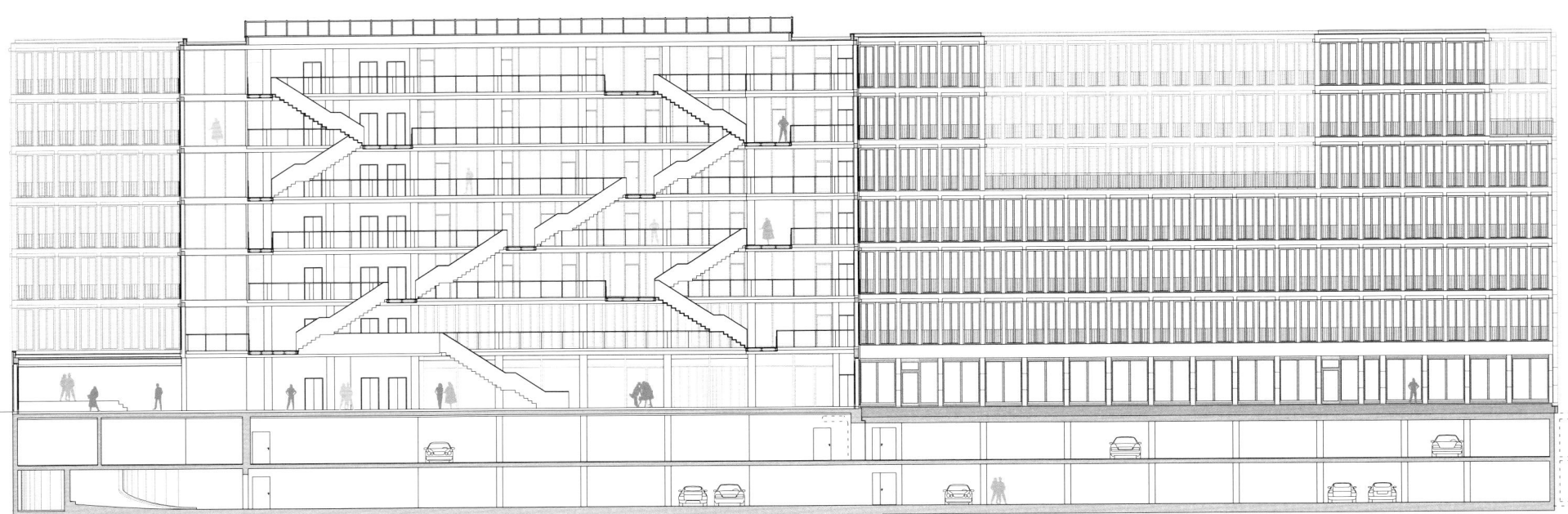

S. 22–25
3–6. Grundrisse (Erdgeschoß, 2. Obergeschoß, 4. Obergeschoß, 6. Obergeschoß).

p. 22–25
3–6. Floor plans (ground floor, 2nd floor, 4th floor, 6th floor).

7. Querschnitt.
8. Längsschnitt.
9. Fassadendetails.

7. Longitudinal section.
8. Transversal section.
9. Façade details.

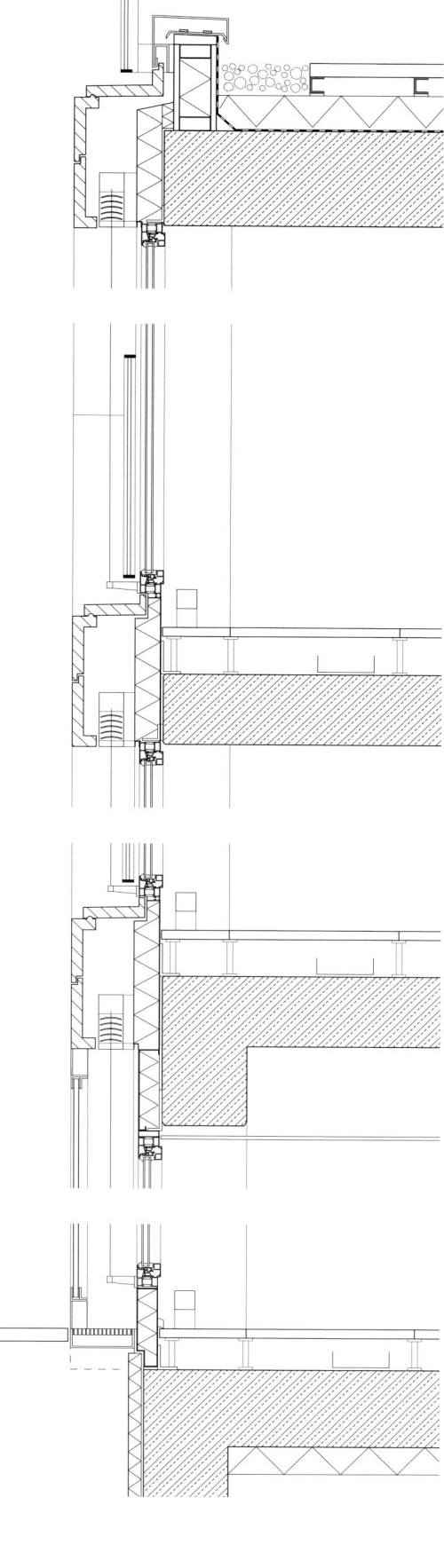

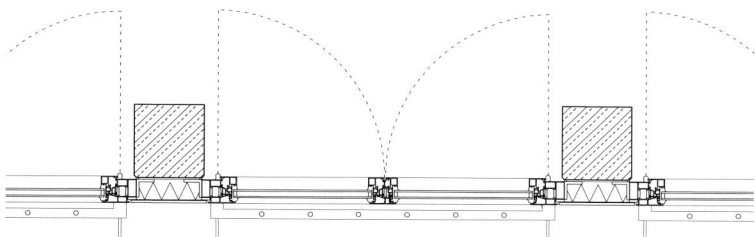

Obergeschoß: Putzfassade
Upper floor: plaster façade

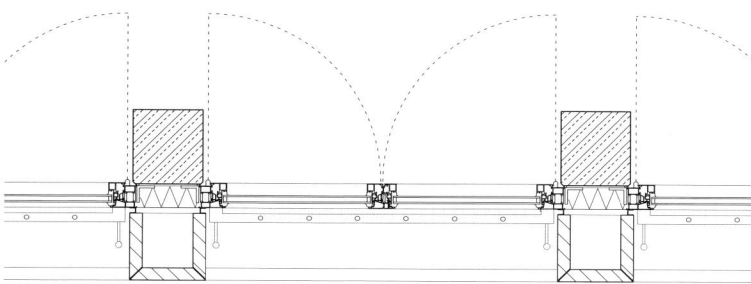

Obergeschoß: Keramikfassade
Upper floor: ceramic façade

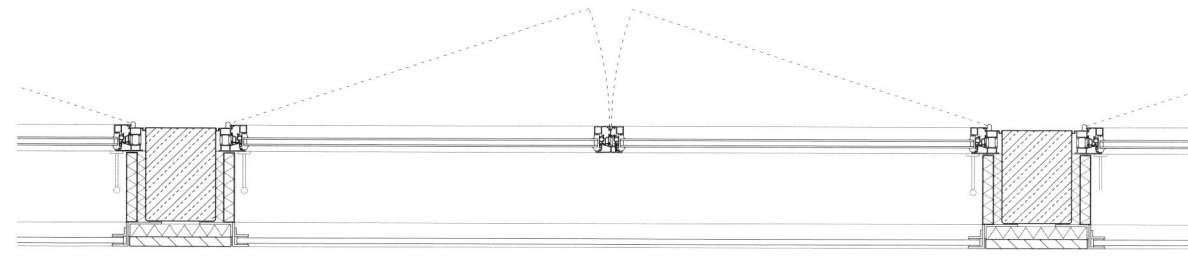

Erdgeschoß: Doppelfassade im Bereich der Putzfassade
Ground floor: double façade in the area of the plaster façade

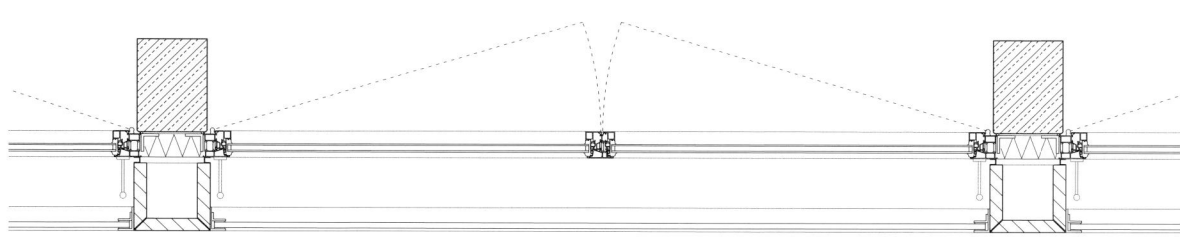

Erdgeschoß: Doppelfassade im Bereich der Keramikfassade
Ground floor: double façade in the area of the ceramic façade

1. Gesamtansicht von Südwesten.

1. General view from the southwest.

2, 3. Detailansichten der Westseite.

2, 3. Detailed views of the west side.

4. 5. Detailansichten der Südwestecke.

4. 5. Detailed views of the der southwest corner.

6. Ansicht von Südosten.
7. Ansicht von Nordosten.

6. View from the southeast.
7. Ansicht from the northeast.

8, 9. Detailansichten der Ostseite.

8, 9. Detailed views of the east side.

10. Gesamtansicht der Westseite mit Blick in den Eingangshof.

10. General view of the west side looking into the entrance courtyard.

11. Detailansicht der Westseite mit Blick in den Eingangshof.
12. Blick von Nordwesten in den Eingangshof.

11. Detailed view of the west side with insight into the entrance courtyard.
12. View of the entrance courtyard from the northwest.

13, 14. Blick in den nördlichen Innenhof, den »Bibliothekshof«.

13, 14. View of the northern inner courtyard, the »library courtyard«.

15, 16. Blick in den östlichen Innenhof, den Bistrohof.

15, 16. View of the eastern inner courtyard, the bistro courtyard.

17. Blick in die Eingangshalle in Richtung Norden.
18. Blick in die Querhalle südlich der Eingangshalle in Richtung Westen.

17. View of the entrance hall looking north.
18. View of the transversal hall south of the entrance hall looking west.

19, 20. Das Bistro auf der Ostseite des Gebäudes im Erdgeschoß.

19, 20. The bistro at the east side of the building. on the ground floor.

21. Blick in zwei der kleineren Konferenzräume am östlichen Innenhof, dem »Bistrohof«, im Erdgeschoß.
22. Einer der kleineren Konferenzräume am östlichen Innenhof, dem »Bistrohof«, im Erdgeschoß.
23. Der große Konferenzraum auf der Südseite des Gebäudes im Erdgeschoß.

21. View of two of the smaller conference rooms at the eastern courtyard, the »bistro courtyard«, on the ground floor.
22. One of the smaller conference rooms at the eastern inner courtyard, the »bistro courtyard«, on the ground floor.
23. The large conference room at the south side of the building on the ground floor.

24. Die Eingangshalle in Richtung Norden.
25. Detailansicht der Treppenanlage in der Eingangshalle.

24. The entrance hall looking north.
25. Detailed view of the flight of stairs in the entrance hall.

S. 54/55
26. Detailansicht der Treppenanlage in der Eingangshalle.

p. 54/55
26. Detailed view of the flight of stairs in the entrance hall.

S. 56/57
27. Das obere Ende der Treppenanlage in der Eingangshalle.

p. 56/57
27. The top end of the flight of stairs in the entrance hall.

28. Blick von der Treppenanlage in der Eingangshalle in die Büros.
29, 30. Blick in zwei verschiedene Bürobereiche.

28. View of the offices from the flight of stairs in the entrance hall.
29, 30. View of two different office areas.

**KPMG-Gebäude
Ganghoferstraße 29
80339 München**

Entwurfszeit / Design period
1997–1999

Bauzeit / Construction period
1999–2002

Bauherr / Client
KPMG Deutsche Treuhand-Gesellschaft Aktiengesellschaft Wirtschaftsprüfungsgesellschaft (Projektleiter / project manager: Peter Saager)

Architekten / Architects
Workshop: Steidle + Partner, München / Munich (Otto Steidle, Johann Spengler, Johannes Ernst, Tom Repper, Audrey Shimomoura, Michael Guggenbichler)
Realisation / Realization: Steidle + Partner, München / Munich (Projektarchitekten / project architects: Otto Steidle, Johann Spengler; Mitarbeiter / collaborators: Tom Kristen, Tom Repper, Michael Kremsreiter, Stefan Resch, Siegwart Geiger, Christoph Wand)

Farbkonzept / Colour concept
Erich Wiesner, Berlin

Lichtinstallation / Light installation
Ingo Maurer, München / Munich (Ingo Maurer mit / with Heike Dewald, Sebastian Utermöhlen, Bernhard Dessecker, Mathias Liedke

Landschaftsplanung / Landscape planning
Auböck + Kárász, Wien / Vienna (Maria Auböck, János Kárász; Mitarbeiterin / collaborator: Ursula Wieser-Benedetti)

Tragwerksplanung / Structural engineering
CBP Cronauer Beratung Planung Beratende Ingenieure GmbH, München / Munich (Projektleiter / project manager: Winnhard Heigl)

Haustechnik / Mechanical engineering
Ing.-Büro Hausladen GmbH, München / Munich (Projektleiter / project manager: Herbert Tremmel)

Generalübernehmer / Project manager and developer
Investa Projektentwicklungs- und Verwaltungs GmbH, München / Munich (Projektleiter / project manager: Jürgen Limpert)

Generalunternehmer / General contractor
Arbeitsgemeinschaft Alte Messe – MK5 – KPMG: Hochtief Construction AG, Niederlassung München (Projektleiter / project manager: Johann Geber); Siemens Gebäudetechnik Bayern GmbH & Co. OHG, München / Munich (Projektleiter / project manager: Christoph Meier)

Die folgenden Firmen haben die Herausgabe dieses Buches finanziell unterstützt:
The following firms have given financial support to the publication of this book:

KPMG Deutsche Treuhand-Gesellschaft Aktiengesellschaft Wirtschaftsprüfungsgesellschaft

Investa Projektentwicklungs- und Verwaltungs GmbH, München / Munich

CBP Cronauer Beratung Planung Beratende Ingenieure GmbH, München / Munich

Hochtief Construction AG, Niederlassung München

NBK Baukeramik GmbH & Co. KG, Emmerich (Hersteller der Keramikelemente / manufacturer of the ceramic elements)

Strähle Raum-Systeme GmbH, Waiblingen (Hersteller der Glastrennwände / manufacturer of the glass partition walls)

Louis Poulsen & Co. GmbH, Hilden (Hersteller der Decken- und Stehleuchten / manufacturer of the ceiling and floor lamps)